TALES FROM THE YPSILANTI ARCHIVES

TALES FROM THE YPSILANTI

ARCHIVES

TRIPE-MONGERS, PARKER'S HAIR BALSAM, THE UNDERWEAR CLUB & MORE

By LAURA BIEN

THE History PRESS

Published by The History Press
Charleston, SC 29403
www.historypress.net

Cover images courtesy of Ypsilanti Archives.

First published 2010

Manufactured in the United States

ISBN 978.1.59629.877.4

Bien, Laura.
Tales from the Ypsilanti archives : tripe mongers and the underwear club / Laura Bien.
p. cm.
ISBN 978-1-59629-877-4
1. Ypsilanti (Mich.)--History--Anecdotes. 2. Ypsilanti (Mich.)--Social life and customs--Anecdotes. I. Title.
F574.Y8B54 2010
977.4'35--dc22
2009050448

Notice: The information in this book is true and complete to the best of our knowledge. It is offered without guarantee on the part of the author or The History Press. The author and The History Press disclaim all liability in connection with the use of this book.

For Fritz

Contents

FOREWORD

Take a drive up North Huron Street in Ypsilanti, Michigan. The historic buildings that line the street were built in the 1800s. Each has a story to tell, if only we could hear it.

Laura Bien gives these buildings and all of Ypsilanti a voice in *Tales from the Ypsilanti Archives*. Bien mines fascinating bits of history from Ypsilanti's historical archives that illustrate well the parallels between the issues of today and those of yesterday. The stories of the people of Ypsilanti—the loss of a job in the early 1900s when the Ypsilanti Underwear factory closed, the shared struggles of the 1930s Great Depression, the fears of a nuclear attack in the 1960s—are challenges that we can understand at the beginning of the twenty-first century. Other stories deal with the lighter side of life: food, cars, politics, technology, fashion, advertising, Ypsilanti High School colors and even household appliances. Bien's tales of long ago are emblematic of the spirit of Ypsilanti, and they remind us that this spirit lives on today.

After reading *Tales from the Ypsilanti Archives*, you'll be able to drive along North Huron Street and hear the historic buildings telling their stories. Perhaps you'll even get some good advice.

Paul Schreiber
Mayor
Ypsilanti, Michigan

ACKNOWLEDGEMENTS

Grateful thanks are due to Austen Smith at the *Ypsilanti Courier*, Dan Duchene at the *Ypsilanti Citizen*, John Hilton at the *Ann Arbor Observer* and Ed Vielmetti at www.annarbor.com, in whose publications' pages these stories originally appeared. Thanks are also due to Kristin Perkins for her generous loan of Bertha Wiederhoft's letter, to Mayor Schreiber, to Ypsilanti Historical Society president Al Rudisill, to Ypsilanti Archivist Gerry Pety and to the staff of the Ypsilanti Archives.

Part I

Old Times

Ypsilanti Had Its Own Time Zone in 1883

You have to love a city that creates, out of sheer cussedness, its own time zone. That was Ypsilanti from 1883 to at least 1904.

In the early 1880s, communities observed "local time," also called "sun time." Towns and cities gauged time by taking a measurement of the sun's position. They set this time on a highly visible clock in town, such as a church clock. Townspeople set their timepieces by the church clock. However, due to varying sun measurements, clock time differed from town to town, which made it frustrating and expensive for railroads trying to maintain efficient schedules. In 1883, the heads of the big railroad companies met in Chicago and agreed to adopt standard time, with four continental time zones, as their preferred system, in order to regulate their train schedules. Soon afterward, individual states began to copy the railroads' time scheme.

Michigan adopted standard time on September 19, 1885. The legislative decision read, "The People of the State of Michigan enact that standard time, central division, based on the ninetieth meridian of longitude west from Greenwich, shall be legal time within this state."

Ypsilanti simply ignored this state edict. With a few exceptions around town, the city stuck to local time and refused to adopt standard time. And it refused it officially—at an October 1885 city council meeting, the council voted to reject, denounce and squash standard time!

The editor of the *Ypsilanti Commercial* newspaper, C.R. Pattison, approved, calling the council's action "sensible" in the October 24, 1885 paper. Pattison was an ardent temperance man and the author of regular and fiery *Commercial* editorials railing against liquor. The notion of standard time similarly aroused his ire. He said in his paper, "The Common Council has no more business to direct our clocks than to direct when the people shall get up in the morning." He added, "Standard time is a libel upon truth—a standing lie. It is calling a thing that which it is not, never can be, and never ought to be." Gathering momentum, he thundered, "When our people want standard time, they will say so. As yet, nine-tenths are opposed."

One's sympathies go out to the brave one-tenth of Ypsilantians who dared to whisper their support for this reviled plan.

In the October 24, 1885 *Commercial*, Pattison said, "The [Ann Arbor] University runs on standard time next week. The new clock will be placed in the Library tower by November 1st, after which time bells in the tower will chime the hours." In this era's heterogenous style of news story arrangement, that tidbit appeared between an ad for a minstrel show at the Ypsilanti Opera House, a report on the Ypsilanti Cricket Club's match against the Windsor team and a positive review of Bob Burdette's recent talk at University Hall, "The Rise and Fall of the Mustache."

But Pattison's calm tone did not last. In the same edition of the paper, he boomed, "There never was anything more absurd than to foist upon the people standard time. If adopted, every time the town clock struck it would echo over the city an infamous lie. Enough demoralization afloat now, than to add another to mystify, and learn our children falsehood." Standard time had become, according to Pattison, an issue of morality.

Two weeks later, Pattison had not wearied of this topic. He said in the November 7, 1885 *Commercial*, "Sun or normal time has been the standard in all ages of the world, by all nations, civilized and uncivilized." Not burdened with pesky supporting evidence, his argument continued, "[Local time] is the best in accord with reason and common sense."

Detroiters thought so, too, and stuck with local time, while Ann Arbor converted to standard time. The discrepancy between Detroit and Ypsilanti local time and Ann Arbor standard time created confusion on the printed schedules of the interurban streetcars connecting these cities—if one forgot that local time was twenty-eight minutes ahead of standard time.

Despite the state law and the conversion of Ann Arbor, Ypsilanti did not relent. As late as 1904—a generation after the original Michigan law—much of the city still refused to convert to standard time, although other parts did.

The result was a mishmash of confusion, as noted in the May 2, 1904 *Ypsilanti Evening Press*, in a story headlined "Ypsilanti Has Two Kinds of Time":

> *Ypsilanti is run on standard time nominally, actually it is run on any old time that happens to be convenient…for instance, the churches run on local time, but the schools on standard, the theater opens on standard time, but the chief patrons of this place of amusement are people whose day ends and begins by local time…*
>
> *There are some peculiar situations in the city also due to these conditions; for instance there are several places in the city where two business concerns are conducted under the same roof, one running by standard and one by local time. This naturally causes considerable conflict among the employees…it is not beyond the realm of possibility to imagine that there are citizens of Ypsilanti who rise by local and retire by standard time in a mad endeavor to keep up with the times.*

Things are easier today with universal standard time. However, one has to salute earlier citizens' gumption. There were some admirably stubborn, hardheaded Ypsilantians back then. They knew just what kind of time they wanted, dangit, and for over twenty years they did not back down!

Desperate Flight: Passenger Pigeons in Washtenaw County

Immense flocks of passenger pigeons, millions of birds strong, once blackened Washtenaw County skies each spring and fall. But those huge migrations ended more than a century ago, as the entire species was hunted to extinction.

Commercial hunters in Michigan contributed directly to the pigeons' demise at an 1878 Petoskey bloodbath, where the last great flock nested—and died. Some of the last surviving birds, remnants of a biological fury once 5 billion strong, were shot in Washtenaw County. A few became some of the University of Michigan's forty-one specimens, two of which are on display at the Natural History Museum.

A third as large as its closest relative, the mourning dove, the passenger pigeon sported slate-blue wings, a rosy breast and red eyes and feet. A talkative bird, it carried on a constant gabble of rising and falling burbles and squawks punctuated by an occasional loud "KECK-KECK!" During breeding season, a flock's gossipy chatter rose to a shrieking roar that could be heard six miles away.

The flights were awe-inspiring. James Fenimore Cooper compared the sound to the "trampling of thousands of horses on a beaten road...like a crash of thunder." Another witness reported, "Our horse...has been so cowed by them that he would stand still and tremble in his harness." At Saginaw in 1873, one continuous flight passed overhead from 7:30 a.m. to 4:00 p.m.

Prized as a delicious and free food, the pigeons nested in such numbers in Michigan's virgin forests that crashing tree limbs, broken by the weight of roosting birds, posed a danger to early hunters. Native Americans hunted the birds with nets and a modified arrow with a flat disc instead of an arrowhead, which was used to knock nestlings ("squabs") from the trees.

Native Americans hunted passenger pigeons for millennia without significantly denting the bird's population. But in the mid-1800s, the confluence of white settlers, habitat loss from lumbering and large-scale commercial hunting—made possible by railroads for shipping birds to eastern markets and the telegraph, which alerted professional "pigeoneers" to flock locations—wiped out the bird in a few decades.

Passenger pigeons fed primarily on "mast," the rich mixture of beechnuts, acorns and other nuts covering forest floors. Sometimes they fed in long lines on the ground, with the front ranks gobbling up mast. When the rear ranks found no more food, they'd fly to the front, creating a thunderous rolling cylinder that left in its wake what resembled tornado damage.

This frenzy also left no food for settlers' hogs, which fed on mast as well. Pigeons fed on farmers' grain, too, and were killed as pests. But the biggest contributor to the bird's demise was hunting for food. The March 15, 1878 edition of Ann Arbor's *Michigan Argus* newspaper offered this mouthwatering recipe for the then-popular dish of passenger pigeon pot pie:

> *Take six young pigeons, have them neatly drawn, trussed, and singed, stuff them with the chopped livers mixed with parsley, salt, pepper, and a small piece of butter. Cover the bottom of the dish with rather small pieces of beef. On the beef put a thin layer of chopped parsley and mushrooms. Season with pepper and salt. Over this place the pigeons. Between each two put the yolk of a hard-boiled egg. Add some brown sauce or gravy. Cover with puff paste, and bake the pie for an hour and a half.*

Even in 1878, however, pigeons would have been hard to come by. By then, the flocks already had been depleted by the pigeon industry. Pigeons were killed for food or captured alive for the popular pursuit of trapshooting, in which live birds were released for target practice. Several million birds were sacrificed to trapshooting—one shoot in Oswego, New York, killed thirty-five thousand birds.

Others were killed in the pursuit of knowledge. Before the advent of wildlife photography, scientists collected many "study specimens," as both a record and a teaching tool. Even John James Audubon shot the birds he used as models for his famous paintings. "It was at the end of the era when people thought the great abundance of the continent was unlimited," says Janet Hinshaw, collection manager at the U-M Museum of Zoology. "I think when the majority were collected for the museums, [the collectors] had no idea they would be extinct in thirty or forty years."

By far the biggest death toll was caused by commercial hunters. In 1869, Van Buren County alone shipped 7.5 million passenger pigeons to market. One tactic hunters used was to tie a live pigeon to a long stick and, from a bird blind, move it to make the bird flutter. Other pigeons would fly to the distressed bird, only to be netted. The stick, called a "stool," gave us the phrase "stool pigeon." Birds were also shot, poked from nests with sticks and smoked from breeding grounds with pots of burning sulfur. Sometimes whole trees full of squabs were simply felled, or forests burned, with roasted pigeons falling to the ground.

Originally populating the southern tier of Lower Peninsula counties, the pigeons retreated north as the slaughter progressed. By the late 1870s, writers were commenting on the "waning flocks," and the state tried to protect breeding pigeons by forbidding hunters to attack their rookeries. But killing them elsewhere remained legal. In 1878, when the last great flock congregated in Petoskey, an estimated 2 million were killed.

The pigeons never recovered.

One flock appeared in Ohio in 1896, and solo birds or flocks appeared throughout Michigan for twenty years after the Petoskey killing. In 1892, three birds were captured in Scio Township and one in Hillsdale. In 1893, a pigeon was shot in Ypsilanti, and in 1894 another was killed in Scio.

In 1897, a passenger pigeon was spotted among tame pigeons in Sault Ste. Marie. In 1898, a flock was spotted in Washtenaw County. In 1902, two birds were heard to "holler" in the northern Lower Peninsula.

In 1930, a witness reported seeing one bird in an uninhabited region of the Upper Peninsula.

And then they were gone.

THREE YPSILANTI CHICKEN-MEN

The history of chickens in Ypsilanti is as old as the city itself, dating back to the roast chickens served at the first Fourth of July feast celebrated in Woodruff's Grove in 1824.

In subsequent generations, many Ypsilantians raised chickens. But for out-county farmers, one problem was getting eggs to town. Many farmers sold eggs to city grocers, some of whom accepted farm produce to sell. But how would one move, or have an egg dealer move, an extremely fragile and perishable product over washboard dirt roads in a wagon to make a sale big enough to be worth the while?

In 1872, thirty-nine-year-old Ypsilanti resident William O. Strong solved this problem by inventing an egg carrier. He wasn't alone; eleven other tinkerers patented egg carriers that year.

Strong's egg carrier consisted of two square, flat pieces of wood. The top piece had holes drilled in a grid pattern. Two petal-shaped prongs of wire extend up through each hole, with their feet spreading under the top board and touching the bottom board. When eggs are placed in the prongs, and the top board is pressed down, the wire feet are flattened, clamping the prongs around the egg and holding it upright for shipping. Strong had invented a forerunner of the egg carton.

Strong was so taken with his egg carrier invention that he immediately founded a company to mass-produce it. The Excelsior Manufacturing Company stood on the south side of Congress (Michigan Avenue), between Huron and Washington Streets. In 1874, the firm had four employees: proprietor Edward W. Grant, superintendent William Strong and William's two sons as clerks, the seventeen-year-old James and sixteen-year-old Edward. James and Edward lived with William at Congress and Normal, just a few blocks west of their little factory.

Strong's was the only egg carrier manufacturer in Ypsilanti, but by 1878 the tiny firm had vanished from the city, as had all three Strong gentlemen. Apparently, their dream had proved as fragile as an eggshell.

An undated photo from the Ypsilanti City Archives (see pages 20–21) shows the Boston Poultry House, whose façade bears the address 24 Water Street and the phrase "Good Live Poultry of All Kinds Wanted." It stood near the southeast corner of the river and Michigan Avenue.

In the photo, the Boston Poultry House appears to be a thriving business, with twenty-three presumable employees lined up in front of its large wood-frame building. One would not be surprised to learn that it was in business for many years. However, the photo conceals a sadder story.

The Boston Poultry House was run by George H. Morse, a poultry dealer in town since 1897. A bachelor then, he owned a home at 210 River Street. By 1901, he was a boarder in the same home. Perhaps he'd sold it to raise money for his desired poultry house. In 1901, he was also married to Lizzie, who lived with him. Conceivably, Lizzie had admired Morse's ambition to establish his own business.

In 1903, Morse realized his ambition. The Poultry House was open! Proud of his venture, Morse splurged on a telephone, becoming one of the few businesses in town to have one. His telephone number was 467. The photo may have been taken to commemorate the BPH's opening. Likely one of the men at the extreme left is George Morse.

However, things began to fall apart. Though his ambition was realized, Morse apparently lost his wife, who vanished in 1903 from 210 River, where he continued to board. Shortly afterward, the entire Boston Poultry House business was lost as well. The building stood empty and was later demolished. At last, Morse himself vanished from Ypsilanti.

In contrast to Strong and Morse's apparent failures, Eber Owen was successful with chickens. Eber was the son of Ypsilanti's would-be mineral water baron, Tubal Cain Owen.

Owen, who had drilled a well in 1884 and discovered foul salt water, immediately marketed the murky liquid as a cure for thirty-two diseases that included diabetes, hemorrhoids, hay fever, cuts, bee stings, sexual diseases and cancer. He also founded a "Sanitarium," where patrons could seek other cures. About 1903, the popularity of Tubal's sanitarium was declining. His "San" was admitting greater numbers of alcoholics experiencing alcohol withdrawal and delirium tremens. Their yells and screams were annoying neighbors and attracting public comment. When the Pure Foods Act, requiring precise labeling of ingredients, passed in 1906, Tubal toned down the flashy marketing of his miracle mineral water and continued to sell it as mere mineral water. Tubal died in 1913, and about 1916, his wells were capped forever.

About 1903, Tubal gave Eber part of the land on which the Atlantis water factory stood at 714 Forest, now occupied by the old Roosevelt High School on the Eastern Michigan University (EMU) campus. Eber began breeding poultry in the shadow, as it were, of his father's enormous wooden water pump derrick.

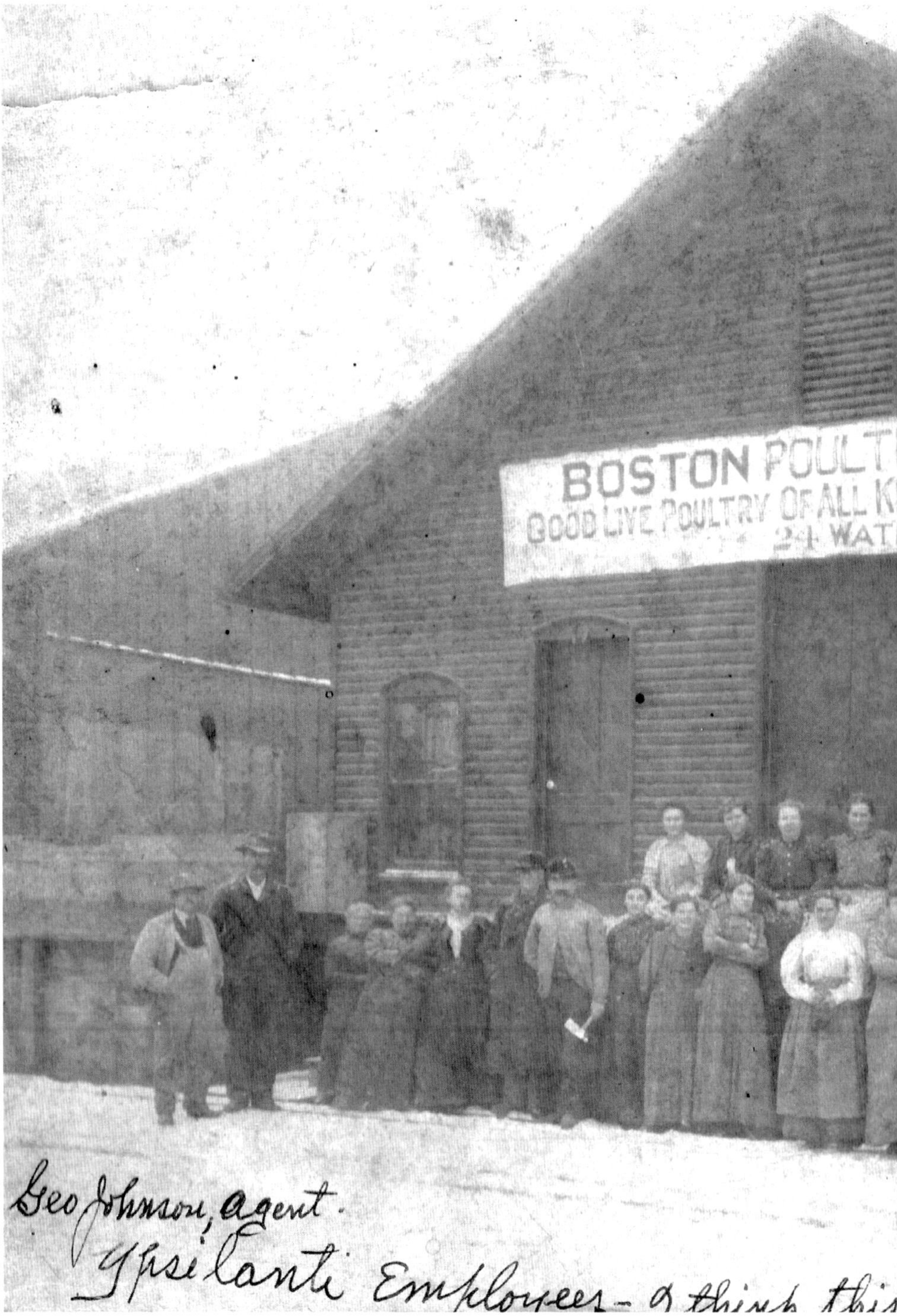
BOSTON
GOOD LIVE POULTRY OF ALL
Geo Johnson, agent.
Ypsilanti Employees

The Boston Poultry House, seen here about 1903, stood at the southeast corner of Michigan Avenue and the river. *Courtesy of Ypsilanti Archives.*

Eber successfully bred and sold poultry into his fifties, long after his father's "Atlantis" well had closed. He brought his birds to local poultry shows, where they won awards and got his name mentioned in the paper. For most of his career, Eber was one of the most prominent poultrymen in the county. Here's a salute to all three gentlemen whose dreams, hopes, ambitions and fates were intertwined with the humble chicken.

THE WANDERING GROOM AND THE VANISHING BRIDE

Courting a sweetie can be an intricate and drawn-out process, full of shy glances, dinners out and long walks. A century ago, one man decided to try a more direct approach. His method attracted the notice of the October 1, 1903 *Ypsilanti Sentinel-Commercial.* "Ypsilanti has long been famous for its underwear," said the paper, "its brainy councils and its enterprising business men, but now it bids fair to become noted in an altogether different way."

Grand Rapids stonecutter William James Pearce arrived in Ypsilanti in September 1903. Five feet, six inches tall with a blocky body and a sandy mustache, he wore a gray suit and a black derby. Pearce walked around town clutching a tiny red notebook. He stopped strangers on the street and told them he was looking for a wife; might the stranger know where he could find one? If, instead of walking away, his startled listener tried to stammer out a reply, Pearce opened his notebook, listened intently and bent his head to take notes.

Pearce crisscrossed several Ypsilanti neighborhoods, continued his interviews and "asked more questions than a census taker and had more nerve then a book agent," said the newspaper.

> *He explained that he was looking for a lady, not a beautiful lady nor a rich lady, but just a lady, and he had matrimonial intentions. He did not care whether she was a widow or a maiden lady, but…* [h]*e did not want a hired girl, as all they would want would be his money to buy cheap perfume and chewing gum, and besides he did not want an old man's darling, but just a wife.*

Reasonable—those chewing gum bills can cost a man a fortune.

Pearce explained, to those who listened, that he was worth $11,000, owned a $3,000 home in Grand Rapids and was ready to give his bride $2,000 on their wedding day. This was evidence of admirable thrift for a stonecutter who earned $4 a day.

Pearce encountered women on his peregrinations and approached several. He told the women that he had a kind, loving nature and wasn't the type of man to swear, drink or stay out late at night.

He also told them that he didn't snore.

Then he proposed.

"[S]o far he has met with marble hearts and icy mitts," noted the newspaper (a reference to a slang expression of the day, about women jilting men: to "give him the mitt" meant to spurn a suitor's advances).

Then Pearce vanished, but not before asking one of his prospective brides for thirty cents to get to Ann Arbor. Perhaps he intended to continue his search there. At the same time, Pearce's son was searching for his father and arrived in Ypsilanti a few days later.

Pearce's son revealed that his father, who actually lived in Pontiac, had been struck on the head six weeks prior by a block of stone. The blow knocked him unconscious. When he came to, he had total amnesia. Doctors decided to operate the next day. But sometime that night, Pearce wandered off and was later spotted in Dearborn, Wayne and Delray. He was briefly arrested in Dearborn but was released. His family searched for him, following rumors of possible sightings.

Pearce's son soon hurried off to Ann Arbor. He hoped to find the owner of the little red notebook that contained kind strangers' impromptu matrimonial advice that, now, would remain useless.

Stony Creek resident George Van Blarcum hurried to Ypsilanti with the marriage license he'd just purchased in Ann Arbor. His fiancée, Anna Belle Throop, had agreed to meet him in Ypsilanti for the ceremony. Van Blarcum had met Throop at a party near Ypsilanti in 1900. She flirted with him, despite being a married woman. Anna told George, a former York Township deputy sheriff, that if he could help her obtain a divorce, she would marry him.

Van Blarcum paid the lawyer's fees. After several setbacks, the divorce decree was finally granted to Throop. "He also gave her money to purchase her wedding outfit," said the March 12, 1904 edition of the *Ypsilanti Evening Press*. "When he was working for the Northwestern Electric railway, near Farmington, and also while working at the Sibley quarry near Wyandotte, he sent her all the money he earned besides what he paid for board and clothes. In all he gave her over $400 on her promise to marry him."

She never appeared for the November marriage ceremony.

The two rescheduled the wedding date. Throop delayed again, citing a different reason. And then again, with yet another pretext. Then she disappeared.

Van Blarcum hired a detective and found Throop in Detroit. She refused point blank to ever marry him and then vanished again.

Van Blarcum asked Judge Gibson to issue a warrant for her arrest. He made an ultimatum: either Anna Belle would return his gifts or marry him—and if she did not marry him, he wouldn't allow her to marry anyone else. The warrant was refused. Van Blarcum couldn't obtain the document he wanted to use, and he couldn't use the document he'd already obtained.

Later "he found her the last time working in an underwear factory in Ypsilanti," said the newspaper. But she was out of reach now. The only thing left in his grasp was one hard-won piece of paper, now useless.

LORA BRYANT: A MIND THAT BECAME UNHINGED IN 1907

When twenty-five-year-old Ypsilanti college student Lora Bryant disappeared in the spring of 1907, those who knew her made weirdly divergent comments on her character and possible fate.

Her father George, a farmer in Dowling, Michigan, said, "I am satisfied that mental derangement was responsible for her going away."

Her roommate Melissa Warner, a fellow Normal College (now Eastern Michigan University) student living at the Hoag boardinghouse, called her "a level-headed, common-sense girl…and not a frivolous one who would do anything foolish."

Oliver Perry Kinsey, vice-president of Bryant's alma mater, Valparaiso University, said, "Miss Bryant's hobby, so far as I have been able to learn, was a desire to go slumming."

Her cousin J.G. Connor, of Millington, Michigan, said, "They can all go home contented. She's gone to the seashore."

Lora Bryant never returned to Ypsilanti.

She hadn't. Bryant was hundreds of miles from Ypsilanti in a Montana slum.

In Helena, Salvation Army worker L.S. Larder telegraphed Normal College authorities to confirm that Bryant was there and to say, as reported in the April 24, 1907 *Ypsilanti Daily Press*, that he "admits the girl told him why she left, but refuses to divulge it. He says the idea that her leaving was the result of an unbalanced mind or of a love affair is preposterous."

Days before she left, Bryant "cashed a $100 New York draft at the First National Bank," reported the April 17, 1907 *Press*. "It was bought in a Hastings, Michigan bank. She drew all the money, something unusual for a student to do." Bryant must have taken the money and squirreled it away in her boardinghouse room over the weekend. She was making plans.

Early Monday morning, Bryant told her roommate that she was going out to gather some wildflower samples for her botany class. Instead, she went to the Ypsilanti depot and bought a train ticket for Chicago from station agent Elmer Mower. When the train pulled away from the platform shortly after 9:00 a.m., Bryant was aboard.

That afternoon, she arrived in Chicago. She stayed one night, and the next morning she bought another train ticket, to Dickinson, North Dakota. A girlfriend of Bryant's, who had graduated from Valparaiso with her, lived there.

Bryant discovered upon her arrival that her friend had moved away. During her college days, Bryant had done some work with a rescue mission. Perhaps nostalgia for that experience led her to head to a Salvation Army rescue mission in Helena. Or perhaps she wanted to head even farther but could not, as the April 24, 1907 *Press* suggested.

"Miss Bryant's money ran out and she got off at Helena and appealed to the Salvation Army to find her work and a respectable boarding house." Bryant "has thrown herself ardently into the work of the Salvationists since she arrived here Friday. She has not missed a service and attended the revival meetings on the streets in the slum parts of the city."

For Bryant to run out of her $100, she would have had to spend the equivalent of $2,200 today—in five days. This was in an era when a train ticket from Ypsilanti to Chicago cost less than $8, and a night's stay in Ypsilanti's own Hawkins Hotel cost $1. Even if the big city prices for a Chicago hotel were double that, it is difficult to see how Bryant spent $100.

As Bryant traveled west, searches for her back in Ypsilanti centered on the agent of numerous tragic deaths in the city, the Huron River.

By the end of Tuesday after Bryant's Monday disappearance, search parties had "scanned both banks of the Huron River from Geddes to the water works plant," reported the Wednesday, April 17, 1907 *Press*. "They found no trace of the missing girl." On Wednesday night, Lora's father arrived in town and with Police Chief Gage spent Thursday morning searching the riverbank in the vicinity of Highland Cemetery. On Friday, Gage and Bryant's cousin, O'Connor, spent the morning searching north of the city, as Officer Ryan and two others walked up the river to the Shanghai gravel pit and searched there. Both parties returned at noon, having found nothing.

A tip came in that a girl of Bryant's description had been seen in Highland Cemetery, and nearby footprints were found in a bank overlooking the bayou just north of the Forest Street Bridge and railroad overpass. The large swampy bayou extended north and east from the river, occupying most of an area bordered by Norris Street, the southern edge of Highland Cemetery and the river. The bayou was the result of the Ypsilanti Underwear Company's dam just south of the Forest Street Bridge. The dam extended from the northern tip of Frog Island to the western bank of the river. The water in the boggy bayou "at this season of the year is from a few inches to a couple of feet in depth," noted the April 21, 1907 *Press*.

On Saturday, Gage spoke of possible plans to open the dam and drain the bayou. "If the Underwear Company's dam were opened," said the April 21 *Press*, "it is calculated that in from two to three hours the water would be lowered several feet, draining the bayou. This would facilitate the work of hunting for the missing girl. If the work were undertaken tomorrow [Sunday], it would not interfere with the mill." It was decided.

On Sunday morning, the news that the dam would be opened attracted hundreds of sightseers. "It seemed as if the whole town had turned out," noted the April 22 *Press*. "Reading that the floodgates at the mill of the Ypsilanti Underwear Company's dam would be raised at daylight, citizens began to gather at five o'clock in the morning." The gates were raised at 7:00 a.m. "Slowly the gates were pried up by iron bars and ratchets. The deep water in the dam went rushing and roaring through the opening. The spectators watched the current, hoping to catch a glimpse of the body, if it were raised by the suction of the water."

The *Press* continued, "Slowly the water above the dam receded and by noon had fallen about three feet. A few boats and canoes patrolled the river, and some more adventurous poled their flat-bottom boats into the bayou, before it became wholly dry."

Chief Gage dragged the river for five hours from two rowboats hitched together. "When Chief Gage had finished his work everyone was satisfied he had done everything he could do to find her body if it lay in the Huron River."

On the following Tuesday came the first telegrams from Montana leading to the confirmation that Bryant was there. From Montana, Bryant wrote her father that she didn't want to come home. Her letter was summarized in the April 27 *Press*. "I left Ypsilanti under a spell of insanity. A man on the train happened to direct me to the Salvation Army in Helena. I don't want to come home." The paper said that "it is her explanation of why she ran away from college here without informing any of her friends or relatives of her going, throwing the whole state into anxiety as to her welfare and causing a heedless expense to the city and her family in efforts to locate her. It is not very satisfying to the general public."

Bryant did eventually return to her home in Dowling, accompanied from Montana by her brother Royal. She then went to Battle Creek for a rest at Kellogg's famous sanitarium, "to take treatment for her nerves," notes the May 9 *Marshall Daily*. "She will not attempt school again, either as a teacher or pupil."

NINETEENTH-CENTURY "PICTURE CARDS"

The following selection of "picture cards," or "trade cards," represents the quotidian historical ephemera only rarely preserved. Ranging from pretty dress-up dolls, included at one time in packages of coffee, to advertising cards touting sarsaparilla and snake oil, the items' innocent and charming aesthetics and promotion of what we now know to be useless "medicines" suggest a period naïveté that modern viewers tend to assume they've outgrown.

However, aside from a general loss of the decorous beauty in advertising seen here, the longer you look at these artifacts, the more you wonder how much has really changed.

This roguish-looking Mr. Fox paper doll was a bonus distributed by a coffee company. The doll came with its own paper buckskin jacket. *Courtesy of Ypsilanti Archives.*

The previous owner inverted Queen Isabella's lace ruff and crown by accident. Lines indicated where the doll could be creased to stand upright. *Courtesy of Ypsilanti Archives.*

Hood's Sarsaparilla was marketed as a cure for a range of ills. Note the old-fashioned doghouse in the background. *Courtesy of Ypsilanti Archives.*

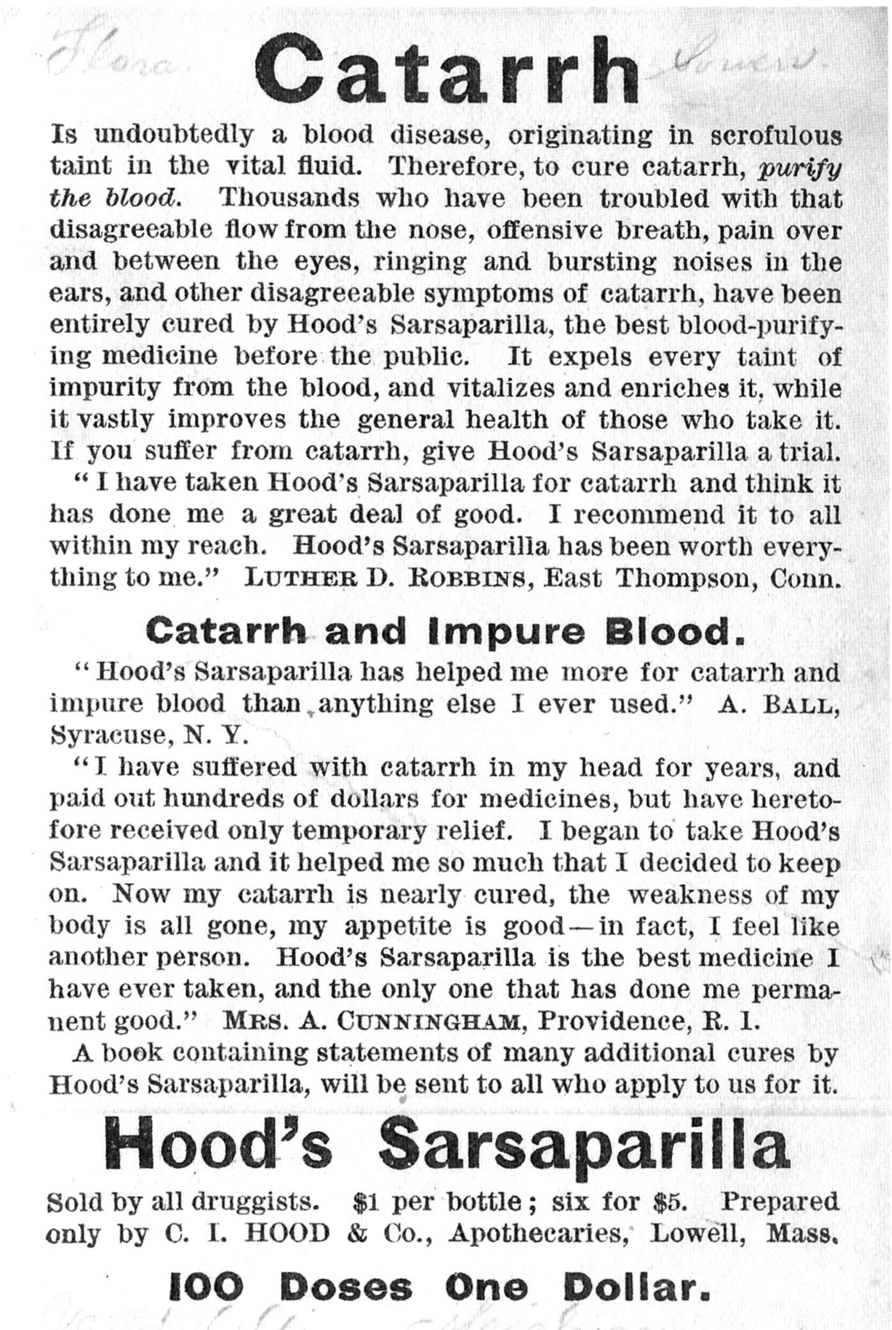

"Catarrh" referred to the inflammation of mucous membranes, especially in the head and throat. *Courtesy of Ypsilanti Archives.*

Marketed as a "temperance drink," Brown's was about 20 percent alcohol, or 40 proof. *Courtesy of Ypsilanti Archives.*

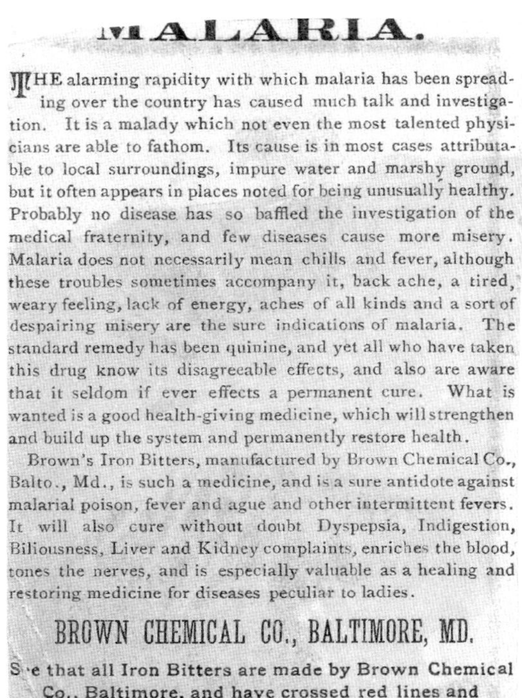

MALARIA.

THE alarming rapidity with which malaria has been spreading over the country has caused much talk and investigation. It is a malady which not even the most talented physicians are able to fathom. Its cause is in most cases attributable to local surroundings, impure water and marshy ground, but it often appears in places noted for being unusually healthy. Probably no disease has so baffled the investigation of the medical fraternity, and few diseases cause more misery. Malaria does not necessarily mean chills and fever, although these troubles sometimes accompany it, back ache, a tired, weary feeling, lack of energy, aches of all kinds and a sort of despairing misery are the sure indications of malaria. The standard remedy has been quinine, and yet all who have taken this drug know its disagreeable effects, and also are aware that it seldom if ever effects a permanent cure. What is wanted is a good health-giving medicine, which will strengthen and build up the system and permanently restore health.

Brown's Iron Bitters, manufactured by Brown Chemical Co., Balto., Md., is such a medicine, and is a sure antidote against malarial poison, fever and ague and other intermittent fevers. It will also cure without doubt Dyspepsia, Indigestion, Biliousness, Liver and Kidney complaints, enriches the blood, tones the nerves, and is especially valuable as a healing and restoring medicine for diseases peculiar to ladies.

BROWN CHEMICAL CO., BALTIMORE, MD.

See that all Iron Bitters are made by Brown Chemical Co., Baltimore, and have crossed red lines and trade-mark on wrapper.

Malaria was once prevalent in Washtenaw County. *Courtesy of Ypsilanti Archives.*

Above: This artist's skill at perspective, as seen in the ashtray, was not quite up to par. *Courtesy of Ypsilanti Archives.*

Left: The back of the cat card. In addition to cards, Royal Yeast also gave away cookbooks. *Courtesy of Ypsilanti Archives.*

Right: Because of their beauty and occasional humor, many picture cards were preserved in scrapbooks. *Courtesy of Ypsilanti Archives.*

Below: This tiny card is about half the size of a business card and may have been distributed at church. *Courtesy of Ypsilanti Archives.*

THE YPSI JANITOR AND THE EMPRESS JOSEPHINE

Many EMU buildings are named for former professors and administrators. But there is no named building, plaque, bench or even a memorial tree to honor EMU's first janitor, whose kindness toward students got him fired.

"Michigan State Normal College [Eastern Michigan University] students never have erected a marker to perpetuate appropriately the memory of the martyrdom of Isaac Kimball in their cause," notes an April 24, 1937 *Ypsilanti Press* story. "It was his duty to ring the college bell for five minutes to announce the opening of classes. Students were supposed to be in the classroom before the bell stopped tolling."

The story continues, "But Kimball was a kindly man. If he saw a student approaching as the five minutes was expiring, he continued tolling. Students became aware of this and depended more and more upon Kimball's generosity."

Things eventually lapsed too far. "One morning, Principal A.S. Welch determined to time the bell. When 15 minutes had passed and Kimball continued his tolling and students continued to arrive, he armed himself with a book, threw it at the gentle-souled janitor, and chased him from the school grounds."

"A new janitor with a heart of flint was on the job next morning," the story noted.

In 1828, at age fourteen, Kimball came to Ypsilanti from his birthplace of Seneca County, New York. He worked as a shoemaker for downtown dry goods storekeeper Walter Hewitt and later as a clerk for grocer Philander Stevens. One day in 1835, Kimball and Harry Gilbert were digging up clay for a house foundation. They dug on the east bank of the Huron River just south of Michigan Avenue, at the north end of the present-day Water Street site. "Those men had not progressed far with their labors when their spades struck timber," says Charles Chapman in his 1881 book *History of Washtenaw County*. "They were not a little surprised, and growing curious, determined to explore this new formation. In the course of their research they discovered a net-work of new timbers; removing one plank they beheld a cave."

The young men carefully lowered themselves into this hidden chamber and found

> *a room ten feet square and eight feet in height; and finally a furnace, half a metal shell filled with a peculiar greasy substance, in which was a wick*

partly consumed. Presently Kimball and Gilbert discovered the exit, a burrow, 100 feet in length, running south into the ravine, and having its outlet in a dense shrubbery near Dr. Davis' present residence.

"This den of infamy had its subterranean location 20 rods [110 yards] south of Congress street [Michigan Avenue], on the slope of the eastern plateau, and was doubtless the hiding place of a gang of counterfeiters, if not of more terrible enemies of human happiness," said Chapman.

The date of its construction cannot be even guessed at. Its builders have passed away, leaving that home of their secret works to relate the story of their infamy and their fall. There is a strange fact in this connection, and that is that great numbers of the pioneers fail to remember anything regarding such a subterranean establishment; however, they acknowledge the existence of a counterfeiters' workshop, south by east of Shad's Hotel.

Likely sometime between this mysterious discovery and 1840, Isaac married a woman named Eliza. They soon had a daughter, Frances, born in 1840, followed by Valiria in 1843, James the next year and John in 1846. In 1846, Eliza was twenty-six years old with four children age six or younger. The family eventually moved to a five-acre farm just south of town, off Harriet Street and west of Hamilton.

Eliza, however, was more than a wife, mother and housekeeper, with farm chores, Monday washdays and three meals to fix from scratch daily. She was also a gardener and experimental botanist. In 1869, she tried to create a new apple variety by cross-pollinating two apple types on one tree. The cross didn't catch. She died ten years afterward, in 1879.

After her death, her experimental tree started producing apples. The next year, it produced even more, and more after that. The fruit was an entirely new apple. The tree was bearing heavily by the time Isaac visited the downtown newspaper office in the spring of 1885, at age seventy, to show the newspapermen Eliza's apple.

"Mr. Isaac B. Kimball brought a couple of specimens of a new apple to the office," said the April 18, 1885 *Ypsilanti Commercial*. "Some sixteen years ago, Mrs. Kimball was in the garden. She was a natural horticulturalist and made many experiments. She shook the pollen of a Talman Sweeting on a Rhode Island Greening, only got one apple from that branch. This was saved until next spring and the seed planted, when three years old set out in the orchard. All but one came to nothing bearing miserable fruit." Eliza died shortly thereafter.

"At the end of thirteen years this one that bore the new apple produced a bushel," continued the paper. "The next year three bushels and last fall seventeen bushels of a uniform, fine size and now the middle of April, sound and healthy. It is fine grained and juicy, a sweet apple and very pleasant tasting. It fills a gap long desired. Mr. Kimball is advanced in years, but would like some nurseryman to take hold of this fruit and so bless the coming generations."

The Ann Arbor Pomological Society examined the apple that year and praised its juicy, firm flesh. They named it the Josephine, after Napoleon's wife, Empress Josephine, herself an amateur botanist.

The Josephine still exists today, blessing our generation. It is known for its longevity in storage, where it stays fresh and sweet all winter, just as memories of Eliza must have remained thus with Isaac, so many years after he watched her experiment with her miraculous, now memorial, tree.

"CABBAGE NIGHT" WAS YPSILANTI'S ORIGINAL HALLOWEEN

"'Hollow Eve,' or 'Cabbage Night,' was celebrated Wednesday night in a wondrous manner," said the November 3, 1877 *Ypsilanti Commercial*. "Several citizens, Thursday morning, found their cabbages missing. They were strewn on many door-steps, and ornamented front doors. And silly lovers of mischief…piled all the barrels and boxes that could be found athwart and midway Congress street [Michigan Avenue]."

Though one of our most ancient holidays, Halloween wasn't celebrated widely in America until the latter part of the 1800s. Ypsilanti likely didn't celebrate Halloween for half a century after the city's founding in 1823—the quote above is the first Halloween story to appear in old newspapers dating back to the 1840s.

Originally the Celtic New Year—celebrated with dressing up in animal heads and skins, making a bonfire and telling fortunes—the holiday in America coincided with the end of harvest time. In the fields, not much more remained than a few rotting cabbages, which mischief-makers grabbed to throw on porches.

Cabbage-hurling was about the extent of Halloween mayhem then. The holiday was not yet popular. Only a few people celebrated it with low-key house parties. "Halloween was remembered by Misses Claribel Champion, Leila Spencer, and Mollie Wise at the home of the former, a party of friends being invited to participate," says the November 7, 1885 *Commercial.* The November 2, 1893 *Ypsilantian* notes:

> *One of the pleasantest of the Halloween parties*... [was] *at the residence of Miss Caroline Hay. The house was tastefully decorated, and illuminated with candles set in Jack lanterns. Bobbing for apples, a trip to the cellar for a cabbage, to see what good things were in store for the future, a hunting contest for apples, and carving the cake for a ring, were among the many incidents that went to make the gathering one long to be remembered.*

The association of apples with Halloween may date back to about AD 40, when Romans, conquering Celtic territory, combined the Celtic New Year with two festivals of their own (one for Pomona, the Roman goddess of fruit and trees whose symbol was the apple).

Around the turn of the century, parties began to be celebrated in schools. The October 29, 1908 *Ypsilanti Daily Press* says, "The ghosts of the Tuttle School will be glad to see their friends at a shadow and box social...come and let Mother Witch reveal the mysteries of your future life."

The next day, the paper described a party at Cleary Hall: "Prof. and Mrs. Cleary chaperoned the young people. Jack-lanterns and black cats were used to decorate." The Beta Nu sorority also held a chaperoned party.

The ancient tradition of fortune-telling was a feature of many Ypsilanti Halloween parties well into the twentieth century. At one 1913 house party, according to the November 6 *Daily Ypsilantian-Press*, "Guests were taken into a darkened room where a ghost was waiting to receive them. An auction sale was held, the various articles selling for not more than 10 cents. Peggy the Spirit Fortune Teller was very popular, also the Gypsy Queen."

During the '20s and '30s, increasing vandalism led to more large community parties meant to distract kids from destructive behavior.

"Three hundred Ypsilanti boys enjoyed Halloween night in a different manner than customarily," said the November 2, 1925 *Daily Ypsilantian-Press*, "when they gathered at Pease Auditorium Saturday night for an evening of fun...Two reels of movies were shown...Prof. Carl Pray told stories for an hour, after which the boys enjoyed a pie eating contest and an apple-eating contest."

Trick-or-treating first shows up in the November 1, 1934 *Ypsilanti Daily Press*: "Dressed in old clothes with faces blacked or covered with masks, groups of children stalked about in a threatening manner. They sneaked around to back porches and demanded of the lady of the house, 'Give us apples, give us candy or else we'll tear down your shanty.'"

Though three police cars were patrolling the city that night, things were quiet. The *Press* said, "There was so little doing that Officers Arthur Kramer and Cyril Ray wearied of their tasks of riding continuously and stopped with children on Wallace Blvd. for a 'weiner' roast."

The paper continued, "The only serious damage reported was on Perrin Street where cabbages and tin cans were thrown on the porch of Mrs. Alexander's residence breaking a stained window glass in the door. Street and stop signs were reported missing at several locations this morning and officers are pondering what to do with a 60-minute parking sign which came here from some other city."

By wartime, community efforts to discourage destruction were expanding. "Halloween mischief was held to a minimum in Ypsilanti Saturday evening," said the November 1, 1943 *Ypsilanti Daily Press*, "when children throughout the city were guests of the American Legion, Kiwanis, and Rotary Clubs at Halloween parties in city schools and at Gilbert House. Games and stories and the showing of motion pictures occupied a part of the evening's entertainment…prizes of war stamps were awarded the best and most original costumes."

By 1950, Halloween parties were held at every school in town, but the efforts only went so far. Destructive behavior climbed that year as police responded to forty calls. One car was pushed into an apple tree, and a convertible had its top slashed. Someone was shooting at cars on the expressway. Multiple leaf piles were set on fire, as was a Franklin Street outhouse.

But it wasn't all bad. When Mr. and Mrs. Anderson were startled by an indoor bat, "Mr. Anderson put on a pair of heavy gloves and woke the bat from restful slumber," said the October 30, 1950 *Ypsilanti Daily Press*. He temporarily put the bat in an empty canary cage. Mrs. Anderson planned to turn the tables on trick-or-treaters, said the paper, and show the bat (eek!) "to any interested 'beggar' who comes around to her house."

History of the Ypsilanti High School Colors

A new group of freshmen this year joins the ranks of the Ypsi High scholars and athletes privileged to wear the purple and gold.

But a century ago, Ypsilanti High School (YHS) had no school colors at all. Or you could say that it had eight. Or was it five?

In 1901, each of the four class levels was allowed to choose two class colors. The students kept their class colors as they advanced from freshmen to seniors. In 1901, the freshman class of 1904, with fifty students, chose pale blue and white. The thirty-two sophomores had chosen red and white, and the thirty-two juniors had claimed green and white. The senior class colors were violet and white, and the thirty seniors had a special privilege—they were the only class permitted to choose a class flower. They chose the violet.

Choosing colors gave each rank of students a special identity with and pride in their group. But by the time 1922 rolled around, things were getting a bit too kaleidoscopic.

"The High School colors have always been a mystery," says an article in the 1921–22 YHS yearbook, the *Ypsi-Dixit*.

> *Our football team wore maroon and white jerseys, our basket ball team had red and blue suits, our baseball uniforms were brown and white. In the lunch room was a Y.H.S. banner of red and green felt. On another school banner the colors were maroon and white. Such confusion as this did not permit us to be very loyal to the school, because we couldn't wear our school colors, or wax enthused over them when they were displayed, for we knew not what they were…*
>
> *This problem was called to the attention of the students by the Sem* [school newspaper], *and was discussed in Student Council. It was put up to a vote of the students, and at first it looked as though maroon and white would be sanctioned, but as so many schools have these colors, and as the* [varsity] *letter issued to athletes was gold, the Athletic Council recommended that purple and gold be chosen.*
>
> *The Seniors had already voted for maroon and white, but immediately changed their vote to purple and gold, and the other classes did the same. Purple and gold was officially established as the school colors for Ypsi High.*

A few days later at a basketball pep rally, the students held a mock funeral, complete with coffin, for the doomed maroon and white. The school's Mechanical Drawing and Sewing classes made a big banner showing a golden letter "Y" on a purple background. The tradition had begun.

Today, Ypsilanti High School athletes wear the same golden varsity letter as their brother and sister athletes of 1922, where the proud tradition of purple and gold began in the Athletic Department eighty-seven years ago.

YPSILANTI BEAT JACKIE ROBINSON BY TWENTY-EIGHT YEARS: INTEGRATED BASEBALL IN 1919

Black baseball player Jackie Robinson famously integrated professional baseball when he played for the Brooklyn Dodgers in 1947. In his first season, he was selected as Rookie of the Year. Later, Robinson was voted the National League's Most Valuable Player and led the Dodgers to the World Series. He accomplished all this in a segregated society rife with brutal racism.

Although Robinson's performance with the Dodgers is most people's mental touchstone for the integration of baseball, Ypsilanti had an integrated city "Factory League" in 1919. Teams from the factories around town squared off against one another in a summer series. The team from the local Pressed Steel Company, in the period words of this *Ypsilanti Daily Press* article, was "composed entirely of colored boys" (the white players are called "boys" as well).

The paper described the Pressed Steel team's star hitter, M. Stacks, and his triple over the left field fence, which helped lead the Pressed Steel team to victory that day. The paper gives the stats for both teams and some analysis.

Lest this suggested equality paint too rosy a picture, it should be recalled that in 1910, just a few years earlier, black employment had been generally relegated to Ypsilanti's most difficult, menial and low-paying jobs. With that in mind, it must be noted that the summer 1919 *Daily Press* also contains a grim news article about a black man, accused of alleged relations with a white woman, who was lynched in Texas. It is unlikely that black baseball teams were playing white ones in much of the segregated South of the time.

Jackie Robinson is regarded as a man who helped pave the way for the civil rights movement. But his nonprofessional black baseball colleagues in 1919 Ypsilanti, even just by playing this local game, were doing their part as well.

The Heavyweight Who Fought Jack Dempsey

New York writer Damon Runyon, famous for his hard-boiled style, called him "the old weeping willow from Paw Paw, Michigan." And that's where Ypsilanti heavyweight boxer Homer Smith's career began, just west of Kalamazoo in the Paw Paw Longwell Opera House. On December 10, 1911, he fought Grand Rapids heavyweight Art Watkins…and knocked him out in five seconds flat.

It was the beginning of a seventeen-year career, from 1911 to 1928, that would match Smith against some of the greatest fighters of the era.

The most famous loss occurred on January 25, 1918, in Racine, Wisconsin. The twenty-six-year-old Smith faced off against Jack Dempsey, who was only one year away from winning the world heavyweight championship, a title he would successfully defend from 1919 to 1926.

The match began and the men circled each other. They exchanged a few punches, and then Dempsey attacked with a wicked left jab. Smith was knocked down. The fight was over in three-quarters of a round. Smith earned $218 for the fight (about $3,100 today).

Smith served in the army during World War I. He completed a tour of duty in France, driving supplies and artillery to a training camp, and gave many boxing exhibitions to soldiers. Afterward, he returned to his boxing career.

In 1923, Smith went on to fight 1908–15 heavyweight champion Jack Johnson. This time Smith lasted twelve rounds. He lost. "I went the distance," he said in the April 26, 1968 *Ypsilanti Press*. "He got the decision, but not by a big margin. I thought I won."

The paper continued, "Smith said Johnson was one of the toughest men he ever fought. 'Johnson was so big, so tremendously strong…he was such a wonderful boxer.'"

In the same year, Smith fought Harry Wills in New York. He was matched with Jack Renault and Jack Sharkey in 1924. Sharkey would go on to earn the heavyweight championship in 1932 and defend it for a year. The next year, Smith lost (on a foul) to Mexican champion Tony Fuente in a match in Mexico City with fifty thousand fans in attendance.

Smith never fought the other boxing great of his time, Joe Louis, who held the heavyweight title longer than any other boxer, from 1937 to 1949. But Smith didn't think Cassius Clay (later known as Muhammad Ali), the holder of the heavyweight championship at the time of the 1968 *Ypsilanti Press* interview, could measure up to the oldtime greats of Louis, Dempsey or Johnson.

"I think Clay is a great fighter and champion of the world," Smith is quoted as saying in the *Press*. "But he's not an all-time great. I think they were a little faster than Clay. Louis would probably have beaten Clay…I would put those three ahead of Clay."

The *Press* interview had been held the day before at a Detroit banquet at Carl's Chophouse honoring Smith and four other boxing greats. Smith received a plaque from the Veteran Boxers Association. The other honorees were Charles P. "Chuck" Davey, a former lightweight and Michigan boxing commissioner; John May, general superintendent of the Detroit Department of Parks and Recreation; and Dr. Bennett, a longtime doctor to such boxers as 1962–64 heavyweight champion Sonny Liston and 1946–50 welterweight champion Sugar Ray Robinson.

Homer Smith holds a postcard from his friend Jack Dempsey, whom he fought fifty years prior. *Courtesy of Ypsilanti Archives.*

Smith continued to speak highly of other boxers throughout his life and remained friendly with many. A 1967 *Ypsilanti Press* photo shows Smith holding a postcard he had just received from Dempsey—the man he'd fought five decades earlier. The caption says, "Smith remembers vividly the 'left to the jaw' he received from Dempsey in their 1918 fight in Racine, Wisconsin." In his autobiography, Dempsey referred to Smith as "that clean living kid from Kalamazoo," since Smith never smoke nor drank.

Later in life, Smith worked in a real estate office and earned his real estate certification from the University of Michigan at age seventy-one. He lived with his wife, Mary Beatrice, at 712 Washtenaw Avenue, near College Place, one block away from the water tower.

Fans and admirers continued to send him fan letters for the rest of his life with requests for photos and autographs. "By the time of his death," notes his May 7, 1971 *Ypsilanti Press* obituary, "the scrapbook which recorded his career in newspaper clippings, pictures, and articles weighed 27 pounds."

Now that's a heavy weight to be proud of.

Horses Vile and Faithful

Ypsilanti used horses for work, transportation and recreation for about half of its history. Here are some highlights from that long partnership.

Rampant animals posed a public safety problem in nineteenth-century Ypsilanti, and the 1880 city charter made no bones about it:

> *No horse, mare, colt, mule, jackass, cow, calf, bull, ox, heifer, steer, swine, or geese, shall run or be permitted to run, at large anywhere within the limits of the city of Ypsilanti, or be tethered, herded, or in anywise pastured in any street or alley in said city, nor shall chickens or fowls of any kind be permitted, from April 15 to November 1 of each and every year, to run at large anywhere within the limits of the city of Ypsilanti.*

Even properly contained, animals around town could still pose a threat. One chomped on the assistant city surveyor in 1907. "Stanton Ferguson of Ellis Street, while walking on Congress Street yesterday was bitten on the arm by a vicious horse," reported the May 22, 1907 *Ypsilanti Daily*

Press. "A nasty-looking wound was inflicted. The horse is owned by William Jarvis…[Mr. Ferguson] suffered considerable [*sic*] last night but is reported better today."

One animal caused controversy in town but not due to disobedience. When trucks replaced Ypsilanti's horse-drawn fire wagons about 1920, the firehouse's faithful horse Pat was demoted to pulling a city maintenance wagon. His fate turned worse in 1925, as noted by the March 23 *Daily Ypsilantian-Press*:

> *Pat is dead.*
>
> *Pat? You know Pat. He was the aged fire horse that for several years past has been dragging a street clean-up wagon about the streets of Ypsilanti. Pat's death sentence was passed by city aldermen when they were advised by a veterinary that a cancer had developed in one of his eyes and that it was probably painful.*
>
> *For several years Pat has been the center of more or less controversy. Aldermen have argued that he was an unnecessary expense to the city and should be shot. Counter arguments, having much to do with sentiment, have placed a restraining hand on economical inclinations and Pat has lived on, unaware of the fate that threatened him, and serving as well as any horse could serve.*
>
> *There has been considerable hesitation about issuing the final warrant for Pat and even after his execution there was an attempt to keep the affair quiet. "Yes Pat is dead, but don't say anything about it," was the answer to several inquiries.*
>
> *Pat has a history of service. He was raised by George Corkins on his farm near Belleville. He was a fine specimen and full of life. Fire commissioners at that time were on the alert for strong, fast horses and Pat was chosen. For eight years he was faithfully at his post at the fire barn. Then trucks replaced the wagons and Pat became an out cast. A place was found for him in the city maintenance department and during the latter years of his life he had light duties. He was nineteen years old and his best friends will probably be glad to know that Pat is resting.*

On a lighter note, horses also provided entertainment. When Robinson's Circus came to town in the summer of 1866, its ad described a spectacular show of "120 Men, 200 Horses, and a Grand, Comprehensive Menagerie, consisting of specimens of rare WILD ANIMALS Collected from the Four

Quarters of the Globe." The ad also promised "50 Performers, 6 Original Clowns & 20 Educated Ponies!"

Entertainment of a different kind occurred in 1896, when two spooked horses barged into an Ypsilanti hardware store. "The biggest rush on the street last Saturday was in front of F.I. Carpenter's hardware store," reported the May 7, 1896 *Ypsilantian*.

> *Thales L. Buck, of Ann Arbor, drove up in front of the store and jumped out of the buggy to tie his horses, when they became frightened at something on the street and made a grand rush for the cashier's desk in the store. They executed a war dance on a pile of garden rakes and lawn mowers, but fortunately neither horses nor buggy were hurt. The small glass of the west window was broken.*
>
> *Mr. Carpenter declares that the low prices were what attracted the animals—a good example of plain horse sense.*

Low prices of another sort were part of a scheme to get on Mayor Watson Snyder's good side in 1873. "Several of our saloonists conceived the brilliant idea of stopping liquor prosecutions by means of bribing the Mayor," noted the December 20, 1873 *Ypsilanti Commercial*. "Acting upon this suggestion, they raised a purse, purchased a horse (at auction for one dollar and a quarter—their purses being low lately) and dispatched a messenger to hand over their gift to his Honor, with a complimentary note, which we publish partly as news and partly as a literary curiosity":

> *Ypsilanti December 16th 73*
>
> *Mr. Snider Mare of the Citty of Ypsilanti we the undersign present you with a fine thourbred for a Christmas Present Pleas receive our Complaments also A.W.H. & J.Z.*

"The Mayor was not at home, but his little boy, with true Trojan wit and caution, 'smelt something' about that horse," noted the paper. "[He] ordered the messenger to 'git,' and he got, horse and all. So this remarkable conspiracy was defeated, and everybody rejoices except those who have a 'thourbred' on hand, with a dull market for fancy stock."

Nineteenth-Century ASCII Art

Prohibition movements and laws in Michigan were alive and well long before 1919. The following are some highlights:

> *1790: Law passed that no one residing in or passing through the Northwest Territory give liquor to any Native American.*
>
> *1790: Law passed that no one may sell liquor to soldiers in the Northwest Territory within ten miles of a military post.*

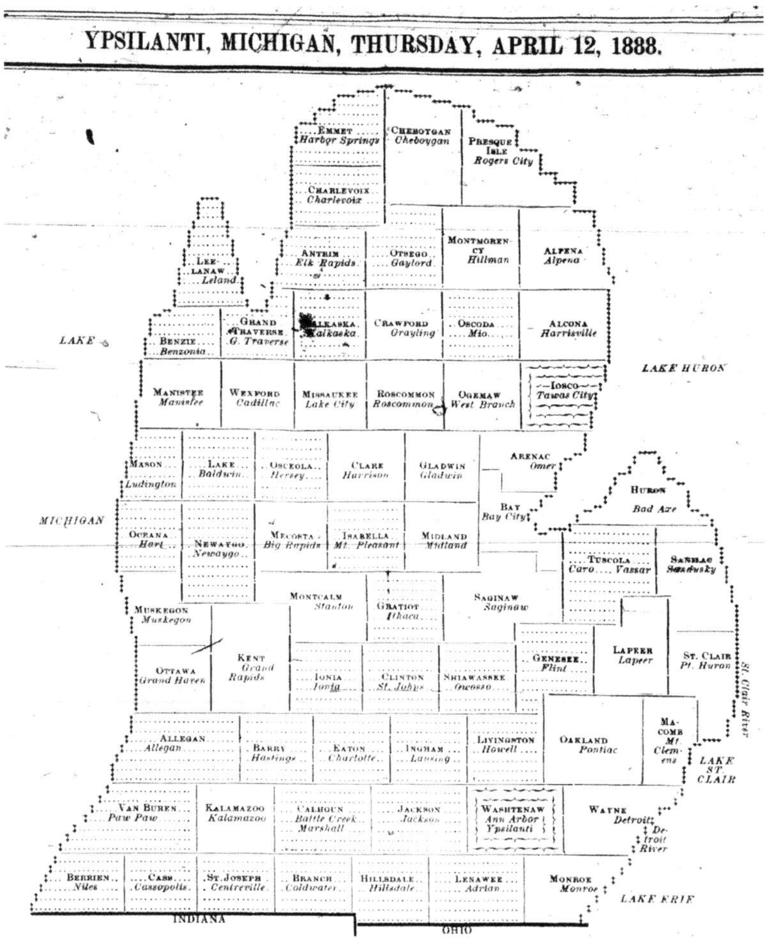

Set by hand with moveable type, this map depicted a Prohibition vote in 1888.

1795: Law passed preventing saloonkeepers from selling liquor to minors, servants, or slaves.

1800: In order to get a liquor license, a potential tavern-keeper must be recommended by "twelve respectable freeholders."

1812: Law passed that anyone selling/giving liquor to Native Americans be fined not less than $5 or more than $100.

1815: Law passed that intoxicating drinks may not be sold to soldiers without written permission of officer in command.

1815: Law passed that liquor may not be sold on Sundays, "except to lodgers and travelers" (day trip to Ann Arbor?).

1845: Law passed that residents of townships and cities could vote on whether to allow liquor in their municipality; this was called "local control."

In 1888, there was a vote for local control. Many Michigan counties voted. So how did the editor of the April 12, 1888 *Ypsilantian* decide to depict the results? He couldn't whip something up on Photoshop.

Well, sir, he typeset, by hand, a map of Michigan, showing the "dry" counties with dotted lines, the "wet" counties with swirly brackets and the nonvoting counties left blank.

This is the single most jaw-dropping tour de force of typesetting ever to appear in any old Ypsi paper. "We found this part troublesome enough to set," says a little story under the map, "and if any printer thinks it a simple job, he may try it for two or three days."

This Ypsi graphic is also older by a decade than the first preserved work of typewriter art, which was a butterfly done entirely on a typewriter by Flora Stacey in 1898. She used hyphens, slashes, brackets, periods, some O's and a single judicious asterisk.

Ypsilanti: kickin' the ASCII art old school—really old school—since 1888!

I Never Would Have Married You If It Weren't for Parker's Hair Balsam

And now, a brief message from my corporate sponsor: Parker's Hair Balsam.

Readers, Laura Bien here. Do you have thinning, brittle or lackadaisical hair? Do you look in the mirror and sigh? Is it pallid, squalid, putrid, torpid

As well as a pomade, Parker's was a marital glue. *Courtesy of Ypsilanti Archives.*

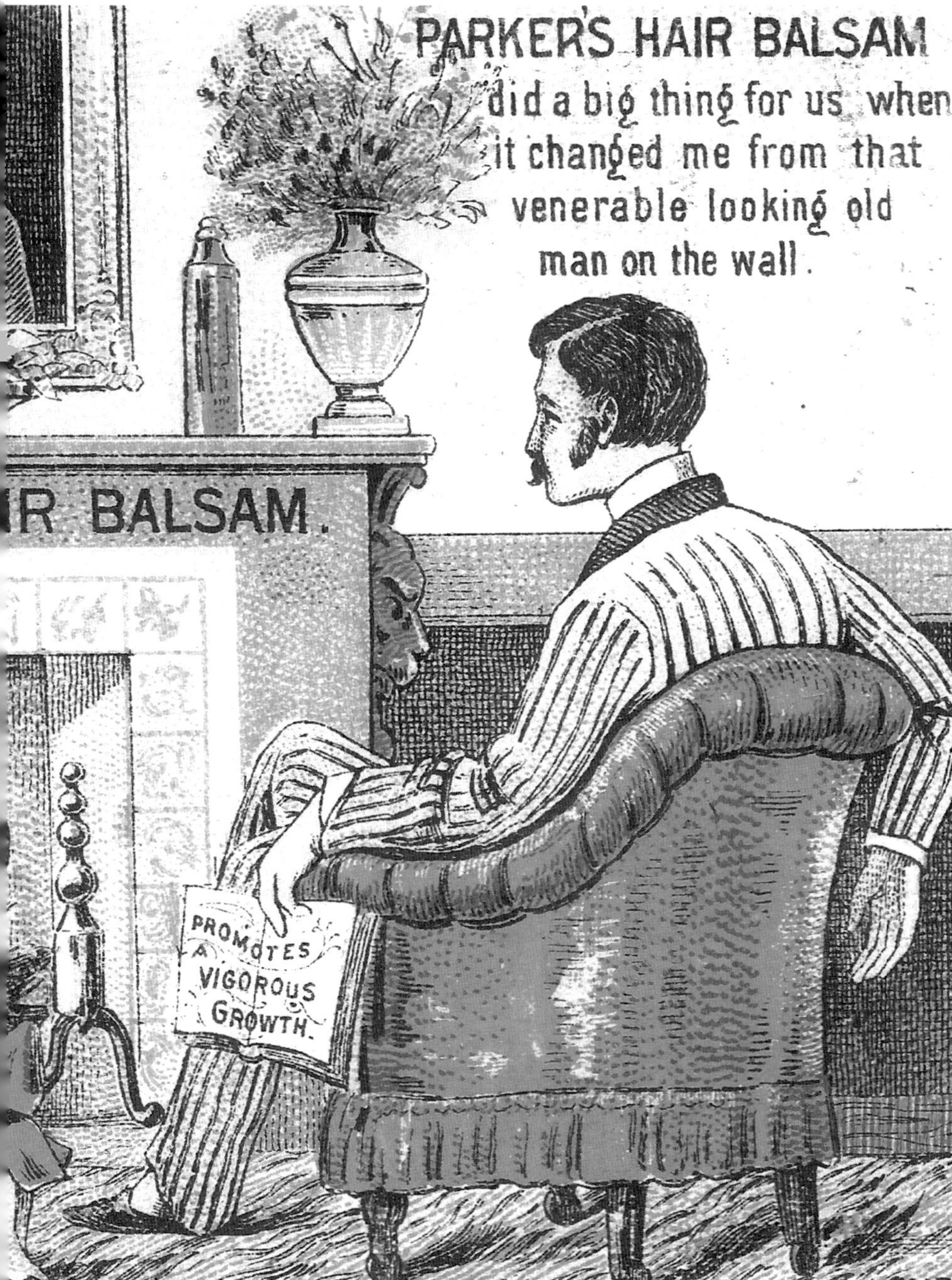
PARKER'S HAIR BALSAM
did a big thing for us when
it changed me from that
venerable looking old
man on the wall.
IR BALSAM.
PROMOTES A VIGOROUS GROWTH.

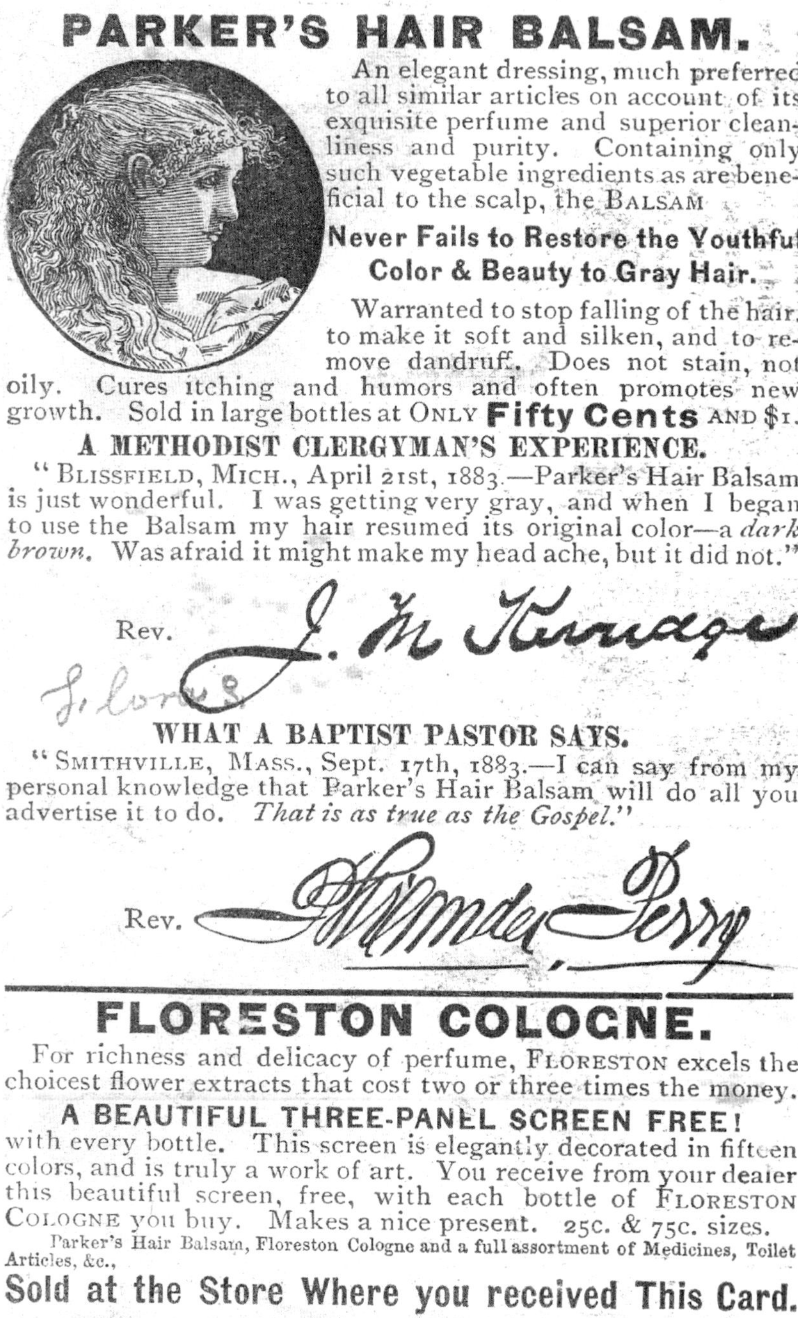

Recommended by clergymen, the dressing had multidenominational appeal. *Courtesy of Ypsilanti Archives.*

or tepid? Are you distracted? Feel inadequate? Not as hirsute as other men? Like to be as shaggy as a buffalo? You need PARKER'S HAIR BALSAM.

Don't take my word for it. Just read for yourself what a Methodist minister in Blissfield, Michigan, has to say: "I was getting very gray, and when I began to use the Balsam my hair resumed its original color—a dark brown. Was afraid it might make my head ache, but it did not."

Of course not. The beneficial vegetable blend in PARKER'S HAIR BALSAM is gentle and bears a sweet perfume. Merely spread our compound of water hemlock, angel's trumpet and soothing pine resin thickly on the scalp (hats not advised). In just days, you'll have all sorts of stuff up there. Remember: PARKER'S HAIR BALSAM. Available at all Ypsilanti druggists.

RIDING ALONG WITH AN YPSILANTI RURAL ROUTE MAILMAN

When the *Detroit Tribune* sent a reporter out to ride on the wagon of rural route mailman and Civil War veteran Lawrence Buland just after the turn of the century, the result was a vivid portrait of Ypsilanti Township farm life.

The reporter said:

> *I have had the opportunity to make the round through 25 miles of zigzag country road with a rural mail carrier, an experience which has possibly never before been enjoyed by a newspaper man, and the striking novelty of the route with its new type of rural roundsman is one that affords a wealth of color and incident.*
>
> *I was fortunate in the selection of my route, as Carrier Lawrence M. Buland, a well-known character in Ypsilanti township and the first carrier on route No. 1 Ypsilanti proved to be a man of fertile resource and varied information.*

Late in October, the reporter arrived at the Ypsilanti Post Office at 9:00 a.m. "in order to catch the rural postmen before they flung their 40 pounds of mail into their carts and beat along the Huron river into the open country in their several directions. Postmaster H.D. Wells with his force were busy sorting mail and the three rural men were found swapping experiences in their waiting room."

The pair set off in Buland's wagon:

> *Carrier Buland is a small, active man, with iron gray mustache and furrowed features. His sharp blue eyes have seen through many a deal which netted him the income on which he lives, for the truth is the carriers get only $500 a year* [about $13,000 today] *and must keep two horses. He arranged his great sackful of mail, threw it in behind the seat of his gig and drove off enthusiastic, hopeful, and full of good nature.*
>
> *One carrier went north, another west, while we followed the Huron river south for several miles. The routes are circular, and no foot of the way is traveled twice in the day.*

The pair left the city traveling south on Huron:

> *The golden beauty of autumn lay over the road, and few people were within doors. Postman Buland rubbed his hands in anticipation: he would be greeted by every man, woman, and child and his leathern bag was bursting. A long line of splendid farms followed the Huron river road as far as the eye could see, beginning at the corporation limits. Here was the first mail box leaning expectantly from its post. Buland's wise black horse spurted in, and the carrier made haste to catch the box on the fly.*
>
> *"She never stops, the old girl knows every turn," said the postman, reaching out to open the box, chuck in the mail, and close the box again. A call from the nearby house brought the mare to a stop.*

This was Hiram and Mary Seaver's farm, just south of Ypsilanti. Mary Seaver was a diarist as well as a farmer, and her diary is preserved in the Ypsilanti Archives. Mary, in her seventies at this time, came to greet Mr. Buland.

> *"Good morning, Aunt Seaver," said Buland to an old lady in a poke bonnet, "how's the baby?" After imparting the information, Aunt Seaver wanted some stamps, and the handy postman doled out a quarter's worth. Mrs. Mary Chicken* [from a farm just southwest of the Seaver farm] *was visiting the new baby. She wanted her mail there. "There was none? Oh, pshaw!"*

For the reporter's sake, Buland asked Mrs. Seaver whether she liked the rural mail service.

"'Why, it's just this way…I don't know what we'd do without it. I really don't know how we'd live if they'd take it away,'" she responded.

Back on the road, Buland expounded on the variety of mailboxes in use:

> *The inspector—Campbell is his name—has not ordered any special kind of box exceptin' that it is rain-proof, which many are not…Now look at that box, not long enough for a paper, and too deep for ordinary diving. When it rains it is easier, as the letters float. They have some large enough to raise a calf in and others if there was a keyhole in it there would be nothing left of box. Some are home-made and tin-lined, and the mare runs on so that I get cut on the edges.*
>
> *The soap boxes are disappearing, though, and the revolving tin boxes are coming in—now there's that flag hanging out without any mail in the box. Some people are careless, though I can't complain. The farmers are good to me. Carry parcels? Sure, if they ask me. But they don't impose on me. They know I wouldn't take money for it. The farmers are peculiar in that way. They are accustomed to doing little favors like that for each other, and know nothing of delivery systems. A farmer would faint if you asked him five cents for taking 10 pounds of sugar 10 miles from town for him.*
>
> *Now, I'm not complaining. You see, they give me little things. Last Christmas I got about $25 worth of provisions and other presents from the farmers along my route. Last year I got about $50 worth altogether. Now, how could I charge anything for carrying an odd parcel for such good-hearted people as that? Besides, they are considerate and seldom ask me.*
>
> *About giving rides? Oh yes, I give anyone a lift. Don't catch me starting out with only one seat. People want to come from town with me. I never refuse, nor do I charge anything.*
>
> *They leave money for stamps and everything. I wish to darnation they would put stamps on their letters. It worries me so to take off my gloves in cold weather and pick up pennies from the corners of mail boxes.*

The *Tribune* reporter said, "The carrier fell into a momentary pessimistic strain of thought as he struck a long uninhabited stretch of road. One could imagine the winter wind shrieking through the great oaks."

Buland spoke again:

> *This road is abominable in winter. There have been pretty tough times with me and the old mare. The cold wind, the heavy clay roads of fall are nothing to that road in winter. For two days winter before last I was stalled*

> *on that road and the people simply didn't get their mail. It's pretty tough in bad weather and I don't mind telling you it's pretty monotonous at times, the same road every day for two years. When it rains I take my top buggy. Some of the carriers complain about the sloppy weather, but I don't kick much.*
>
> *It's deuced hard on a horse. Why, no horse would stand it every day. I have to keep two horses and give them day about on the road. And the government gives me $500 for the work. I start out at 8 o'clock in the morning to sort my mail and don't get back from my round until 3 o'clock in the afternoon. Then it takes me an hour to groom my horse and fix my cart. It costs me $15 a month to feed my horse and $3 a month for blacksmithing.*

Buland explained:

> *I make things meet by turning a deal now and again buying horses and buggies to sell again. I have to give a $1,000 bond and my substitute gives $500. I heard that some carriers in another state were selling things on the side, but that is not done here. We sell nothing and make absolutely no money that way. The express companies tried to get us to act as agents for them here, but our inspector called them off.*
>
> *The road is angular and not the best. The township has spent money fixing up the roads, however, since the rural delivery came in. It is a factor in the making of good roads. Inspector Campbell of this district says we are carrying the mail at a cost of 3 cents a piece, and I carried about 8,000 pieces last month.*

Still on southbound Huron, Buland pointed out some nearby homes. "Weston Bros. live there," said the mailman, pointing to a house,

> *and a fine farm they have. They work the Hammond farm lower down, I believe, Hammond from Detroit, you know, sunk thousands of dollars there, built barns enough to hold Noah's stock during the flood. Back there near the corporate limits of Ypsilanti is S.O. Arnold's box. He lives right next to town, but gets his mail just the same every day from me. His nearest neighbor inside the limits has to travel a mile for it. Henry P. Laflin lives right here—see his name on the box.*

Laflin's farm lay just northeast of the junction of Huron Street and Huron River Drive. Buland turned east onto Huron River Drive.

"By jinks, I forgot to tell you today is the second anniversary of the commencement of this route. I remember talking a while to Austin here on my first trip. I'll call him over. Austin lives on the right hand and his father-in-law on the other side. A better farm can't be seen out of doors.

"Alonzo! Heigh ho-ho! Alonzo!" called the carrier as he flagged Farmer Austin, who was following a seed drill across a beautifully cultivated field. Alonzo came and got his foot up on Buland's hub.

"Now, Alonzo, if you don't like this rural deliver business say so," said Buland encouragingly.

"The rural delivery is all right, but the carrier should be removed," was Alonzo's unexpected reply. Buland wanted to talk about the crops and was further discomfited to hear Austin continue:

"I says to my wife, says I, when you come here first. Says I: 'Mrs. Austin, we ain't er going to like this new fellow that carries the mail. He's a crank. He's a man I ain't going to like.'"

Buland's countenance fell.

"But I reckon I've changed my mind. He's the best fellow in the world and most obliging. The rural delivery is the best thing I've heard of for a long time. Father would not get along without his daily paper now, and I like to glance over it at noon and read every word of it at night. It's as good as a trip to town."

"Dog gone it. I didn't think he was going to give me a bad name, and he didn't," said the carrier, who recovered his composure and in fact was somewhat elated. "Why, he gave a present not long ago some vegetables."

"Here's Frank Stockdale's big crop farm," continued Buland…"He takes a lot of newspapers, two dailies and several bi-weeklies. There is Mrs. M.L. Smith. She is looking expectantly for her mail. They have a neat home there. All good prosperous people on my route, own their own farms, you know. This is the Tuttle hill. E.W. McGrady lives back on the other road, but comes to the corner for his mail. Wish he was around today—fine fellow, and progressive. This is J.W. Tuttle's house, near the Tuttle school. Children ever bother me? Bless me, no, never any trouble."

On the east Monroe road the carrier comes to the Draper corner [at Huron River Drive and Textile roads]. *C.D. Campbell, Albert Day and Wallace Draper have boxes on these corners. Ruth Draper, with 12 years' growth of sunny curls, tripped out to meet him, full of expectancy. The postman means much to her and she has quite a bunch of mail, her very, very own.*

The pair traveled west on Textile and turned south onto Tuttle Hill Road.

> *"Mrs. J.K. Tuttle and W.H. Boutell have the next farms, and they are good ones. Why, here is some money. Seventy-five cents, and nothing to say what for," said the carrier as he fished up a roll of paper inclosing something hard. Three 25-cent pieces fell out.*
>
> *"An old lady who is a widow lives here," continued the carrier as his horse turned in at a cottage nestling under a glorious canopy of maples in autumn foliage. "Mrs. Bertha Bunnaback: her husband died several years ago and she is making a success of farming on her own resources. There was a big mortgage on the place but she has paid it all off."*
>
> *The black mare started suddenly into an open gateway as if looking for an escaped mail box. She drew up at a pump in the yard of the Beamis Bros. farm and the box was on a post beside the pump. The Beamis brothers were threshing beans. An American flag hung from the box instead of the usual signal rag.*
>
> *"We take 16 papers," said Orrin J. Beamis, as he smudged the threshing dust on his face with his sleeve. "We wouldn't do without the daily post for a round sum annually."*
>
> *"I water the mare there every day," explained Buland. "For that reason the box is inside."*
>
> *At the corner of the cross roads* [of Tuttle Hill and Martz Roads] *the carrier came to a school house with a collection of mail boxes. The road here took a turn southwest, this point behind six miles from Ypsilanti, the most distant point on the route which describes a great semi-circle and lies wholly in the township of Ypsilanti. The settlement here* [just north of the border with Augusta Township] *was one of Quakers and prosperity seemed to be located there root and branch.*
>
> *"Four families get their mail here. Mrs. Rhoda Derbyshire, R.E. Gorton, John Groves, and Rev. W.W. Brown. They come from down the cross roads for about half a mile, some of them to save me going up and back. Gorton was our road commissioner. I think most of the people around here are Quakers and they all take a daily paper. When this rural delivery was started there were only two papers taken among the hundred families. Now there are 115. There is food for thought."*

The pair continued south on Tuttle Hill Road to Bemis Road, on the township line.

> *"That fine brick house under the maples is the Alban's home. The Albans are rich and influential farmers. That is G.H. Alban and his brother working by the roadside," said Carrier Buland as he drew up to talk to the busy farmers. At the same moment a man drove up with a jug of corn on a cart. He was dressed in a blue smock and trousers. It was Rev. W.W. Brown, the Quaker minister. His little white church stood on the corner* [of Tuttle Hill and Bemis Roads].
>
> *"Is that you, Mr. Alban? Come here till I see you," called Buland as he fumbled for the Alban mail.*
>
> *"I reckon you're not mistaken, though I'm not much to see," said Farmer Alban as he scraped his boots on his spade.*

Buland asked Farmer Alban about his opinion of the rural mail delivery:

> *The rural delivery, ho! A splendid thing. It makes farm life attractive. You city folks can't crow now. I suppose you'll be wanting to put a tax on us because we have something good. I'm willing. I take two daily papers, and I wouldn't like to be without them. I think we have everything now—telephone and daily mail. I can read the market reports in the paper and no wandering buyer can fool me now with old reports. With the telephone in my house I can sell my produce after consulting the report fresh from the city. I sold a load of grain the other day, and I got the very best price for it. No, sir, you can't take the daily delivery from us now.*

The two set off west on Bemis Road.

> *"Dan O'Brien's place here is just half a mile from Willis post office. He used to get his mail there," said the carrier. "He is the only one who had changed from another office to the route. F.W. Horner, on the other side of the road, is a prominent cattle buyer and takes many daily stock journals. Robert K. Simons, his neighbor, has a box. He says he takes a daily paper to keep up with the system."*
>
> *The carrier got out to stretch himself at the Centennial school, and to make inquiry of the teacher. Her box was perched upon the gate post. A letter, yes, for Miss Mabel Cross, but as there are two Mabel Crosses in the township, and both were teachers, the pretty Miss Cross of the Centennial School looked somewhat cross over the matter.*
>
> *"Herbert Harris's mail box is next," continued the driver. "He is a colored man and an excellent farmer: here are his two dailies."*

"His neighbor is B.D. Kelly, the largest stock raiser in these diggings, and he has the largest mail on my route."

Mrs. Kelly wanted to buy some envelopes, but the carrier wasn't in the business. She said the women folks wouldn't do without the daily delivery for anything.

Fred A. Graves came driving down the road with a load of milk cans direct from Ypsilanti. Mr. Graves was born and has lived 70 years on his farm. Mr. Graves is a very cautious man and slow to admit that there was anything good under the sun.

"This rural delivery is a good thing for them who like it," he admitted.

J.D. Everett, George Crane, and M.A. Merritt, all prominent farmers, were doled out their portions from the sack which was rapidly dwindling. At the Lowden school [on the Lowden farm at Bemis and Stony Creek Roads] *the children sighted the carrier and met him in a throng. The mail for the teacher, Miss Fannie Chatterton, was delivered there, though the little red box was seldom needed. Ex-Rep. James L. Lowden, who, the carrier said, was at first opposed to the system, announced himself as being an enthusiast.*

Carrier Buland pulled up at the house of Newton E. Crittenden [at Bemis and the onetime Ellis Roads], *the staunchest advocate of the delivery in the township. The carrier secured fresh milk at the farm house and ate his lunch while the horse munched Farmer Crittenden's oats.*

"Crittenden thinks our salary should be raised," continued the carrier, as he whipped his horse up again. Buland traveled north on Ellis, which at this time extended south all the way to Bemis Road and beyond. "He tried to have a route established west of here, but some of the farmers are slow to appreciate a good thing."

"L.L. Clement, who lives on the hill here [at Ellis and Textile], *takes the second largest amount of mail. He says he wouldn't take $25 a year and do without it, although he lives only three miles from town. See the old man tottering to the gate? That is Grandfather Chicken. He is over 90, but he hobbles to the gate, rain or shine."*

The old man's face was lit up with a fixed smile as he leaned over the gate with his palsied hand extended as it has been every day for two years at the postman's hour.

"Are you well?" said the old man, in reply to every question.

"I never take the box; the old man's hand is always extended," said Buland feelingly. "And when the weather is too wild I can see the old man peering in at the windows with his still extended hand. I carry him the mail."

"Now, there is the Mowry's, the Ehl's, the Begoles and the Elliott's and I am done," said the roundsman of the country roads as [the southwestern side of] *Ypsilanti was coming into view. "It is 3 o'clock. The last man gets his mail at that hour, while the first not half a mile away got his at 9 a.m. Now, don't you think Uncle Sam should pay us more for the 25 mile route?"*

His listener assented.

The Servant Girl's Letter

One of the rarest types of artifacts ever unearthed in Ypsilanti is an eight-page letter written by a servant girl who worked at 118 South Huron, Henry P. Glover's home.

Glover was at various times the mayor of Ypsilanti, the vice-president of the Ypsilanti Savings Bank, president of the local Scharf Tag Label and Box Company, a founder of the Dress Stay Company and a director of the Ann Arbor and Ypsilanti Street Railway Company. Ypsilanti was his oyster, and in his exquisite home this powerful and wealthy man likely enjoyed the finest of clothing, entertainments and rare and rich foods.

In contrast, up in Glover's dormer-room servant's quarters, his domestic servant Bertha Charlotte Wiederhoft looked forward to her widowed mom's dinner of potato pancakes.

Bertha wrote her friend Emma in Canton, "I cant hardly wait till supper as mother is baking potato pan cakes I can taste them now you probably know how they taste so I won't have to tell you." Later in the letter, Bertha added, "Say Emma I have just got through with my supper + the Pototas Pan Cakes were fine + ate so much that I can hardly write."

Bertha's widowed German mother, Eva, had lost two of her ten children when they were under one year old. Eva's handsome German husband, Frederick, died in 1903. Bertha's sisters also worked as domestics, including her school-aged younger sister, Mary.

Bertha's spelling, sentence structure, punctuation, handwriting and extremely limited interests hint that she, perhaps like Mary, was forced to leave school in order to help support her mom and siblings. Judge for yourself. Here is the letter's transcription:

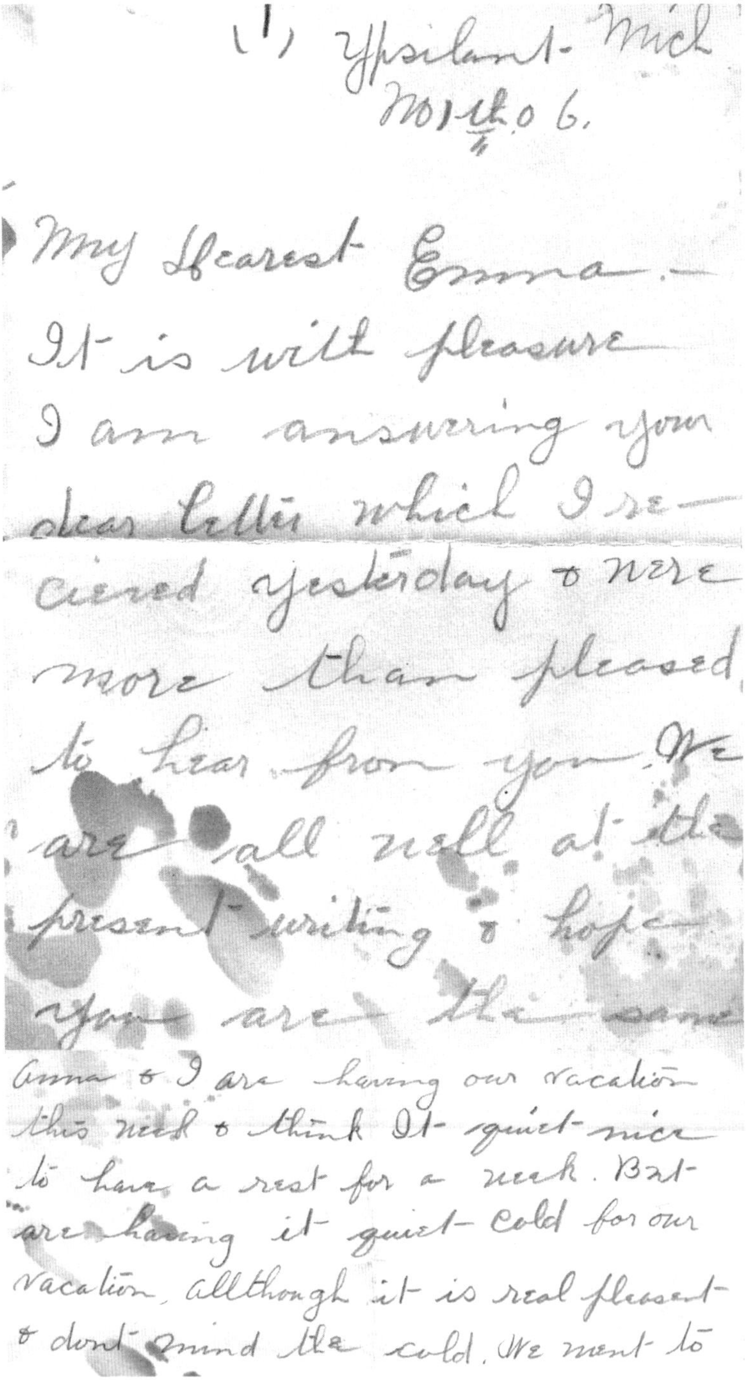

(1) Ypsilant- Mich
Nov 4th 06.

My Dearest Emma.—
It is with pleasure
I am answering your
dear letter which I re-
cieved yesterday & were
more than pleased
to hear from you. We
are all well at the
present writing & hope
you are the same
Emma & I are having our vacation
this week & think It quiet nice
to have a rest for a week. But
are having it quiet cold for our
vacation, allthough it is real pleasant
& dont mind the cold. We went to

This and the following five pages: Bertha Wiederhoft's letter to her friend Emma. *Courtesy of Kristin Perkins.*

Ann Arbor Tuesday to Ida's & had a
very pleasant time had much fun
with the baby. & yesterday we went
out in the Country to
my Cousions on the
Smith farm & spent
the day there & had
a nice time & today
we stayed at home
as I wanted to do some
sewing. I made a waist
for myself monday &
finished it today so you
see I am quiet smart
I wish you were here
just this minute Mary
is just acting up terrible
I Cant hardly wait till

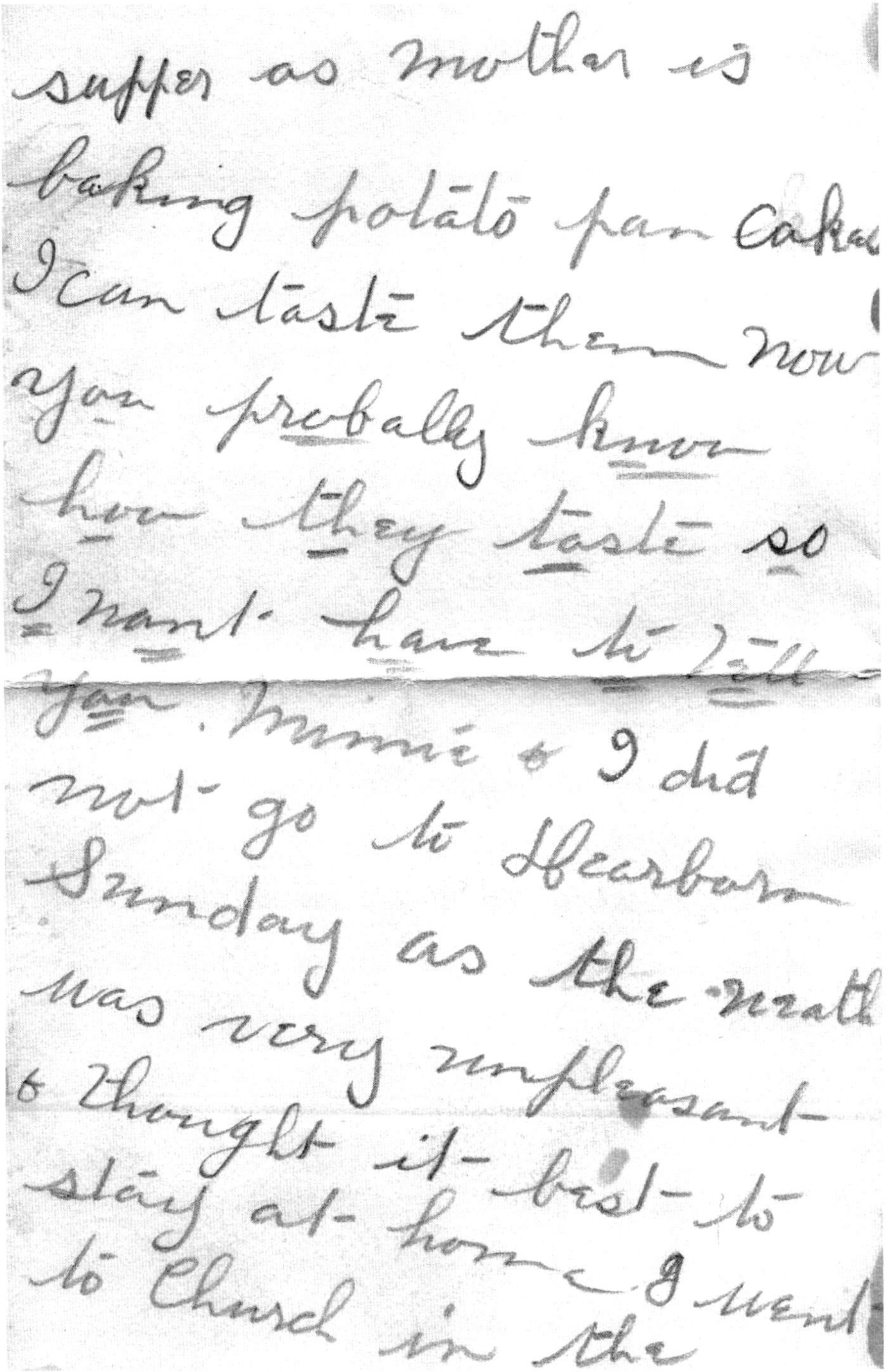

suffer as mother is
baking potato pan cakes
I can taste them now
you probably know
how they taste so
I want have to tell
you. Minnie & I did
not go to Dearborn
Sunday as the weath
was very unpleasant
& thought it best to
stay at home I went
to Church in the

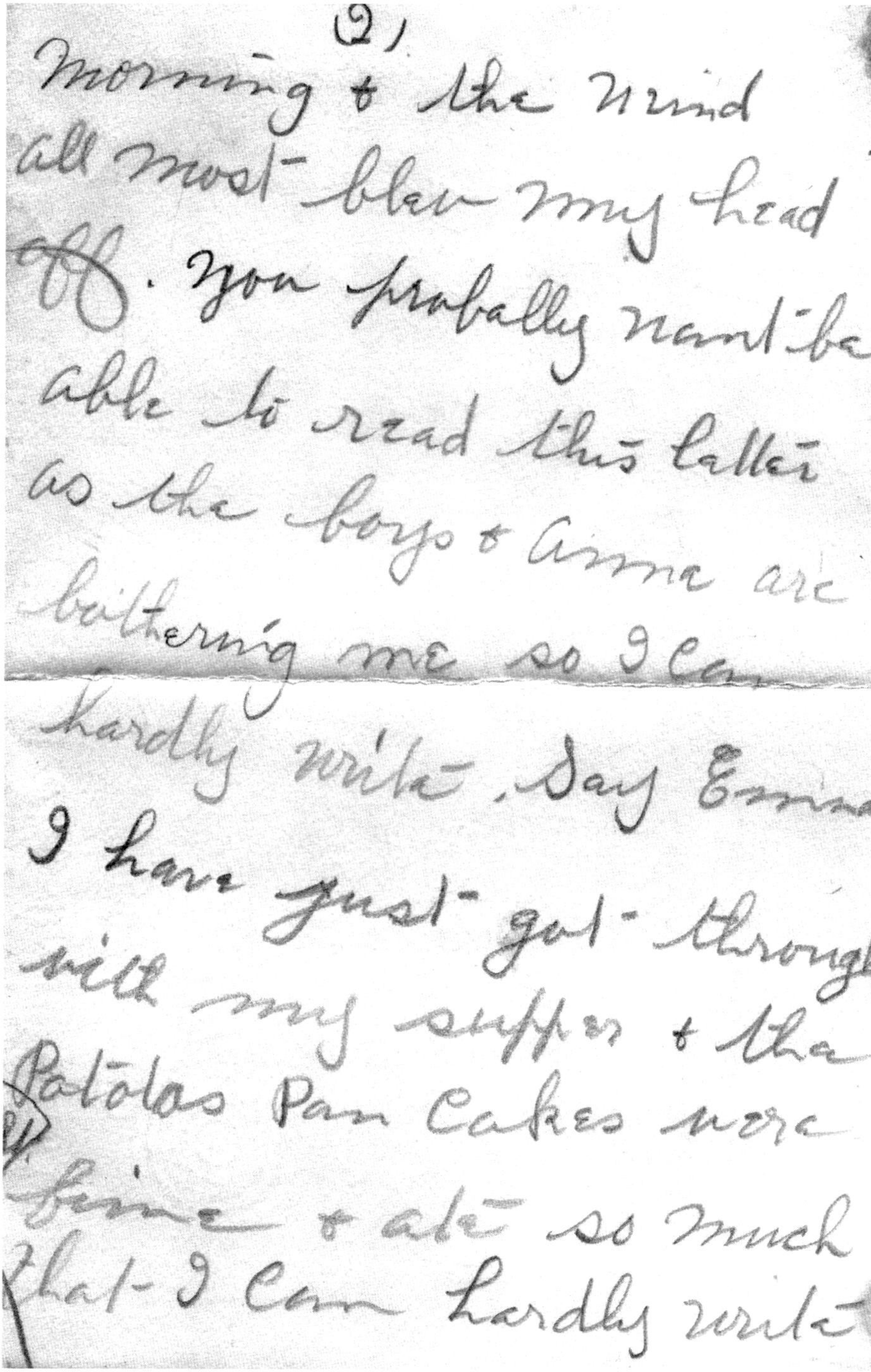

(2)
morning & the wind
all most blew my head
off. You probally wont be
able to read this letter
as the boys & Anna are
bothering me so I can
hardly write. Say Emma
I have just got through
with my supper & the
Potatos Pan Cakes were
fine & ate so much
that I can hardly write

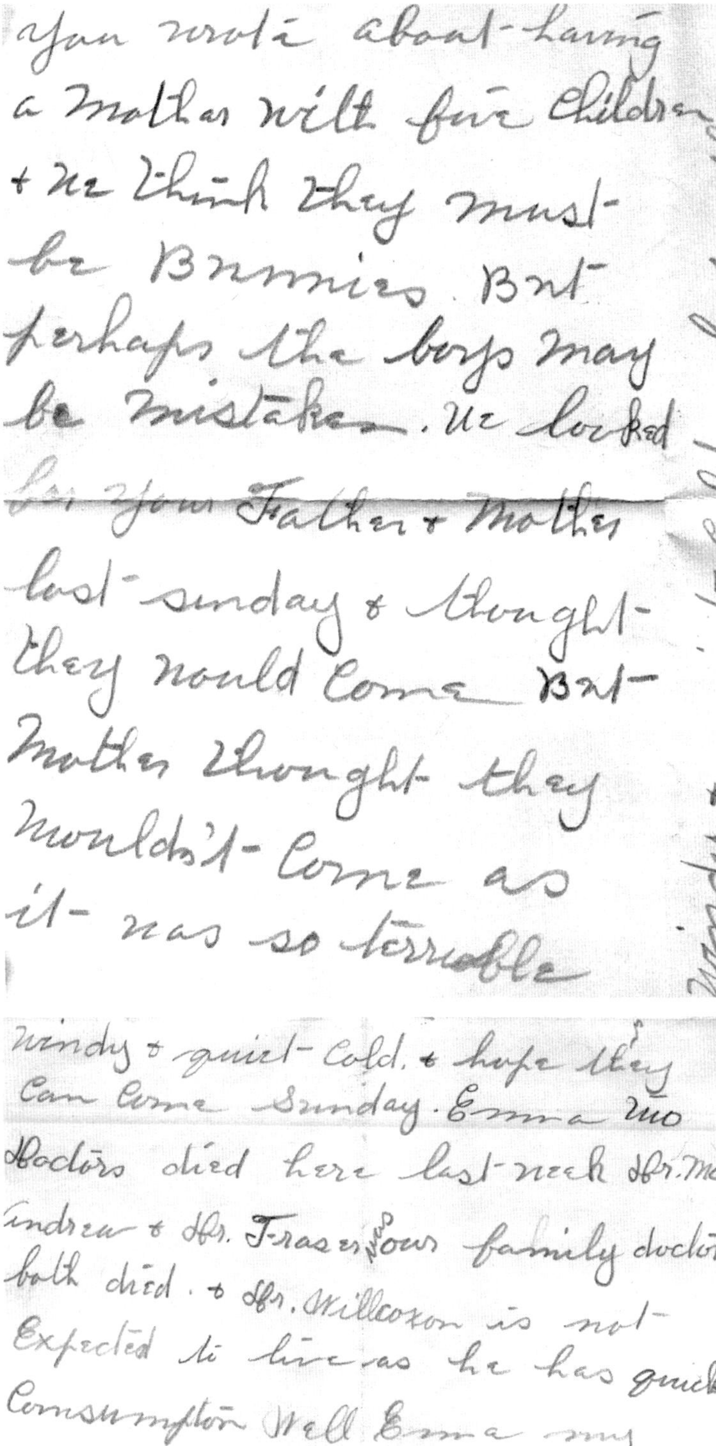

you wrote about having
a Mother with five Children
& we think they must
be Brownies. But
perhaps the boys may
be mistaken. we looked
for your Father & Mother
last sunday & thought
they would come But
Mother thought they
wouldn't come as
it was so terrible
windy & quiet cold. & hope they
Can come Sunday. Emma two
doctors died here last week Dr. Mc
andrew & Dr. Fraser was our family doctor
both died. & Dr. Willcoxon is not
Expected to live as he has quick
Consumption Well Emma say

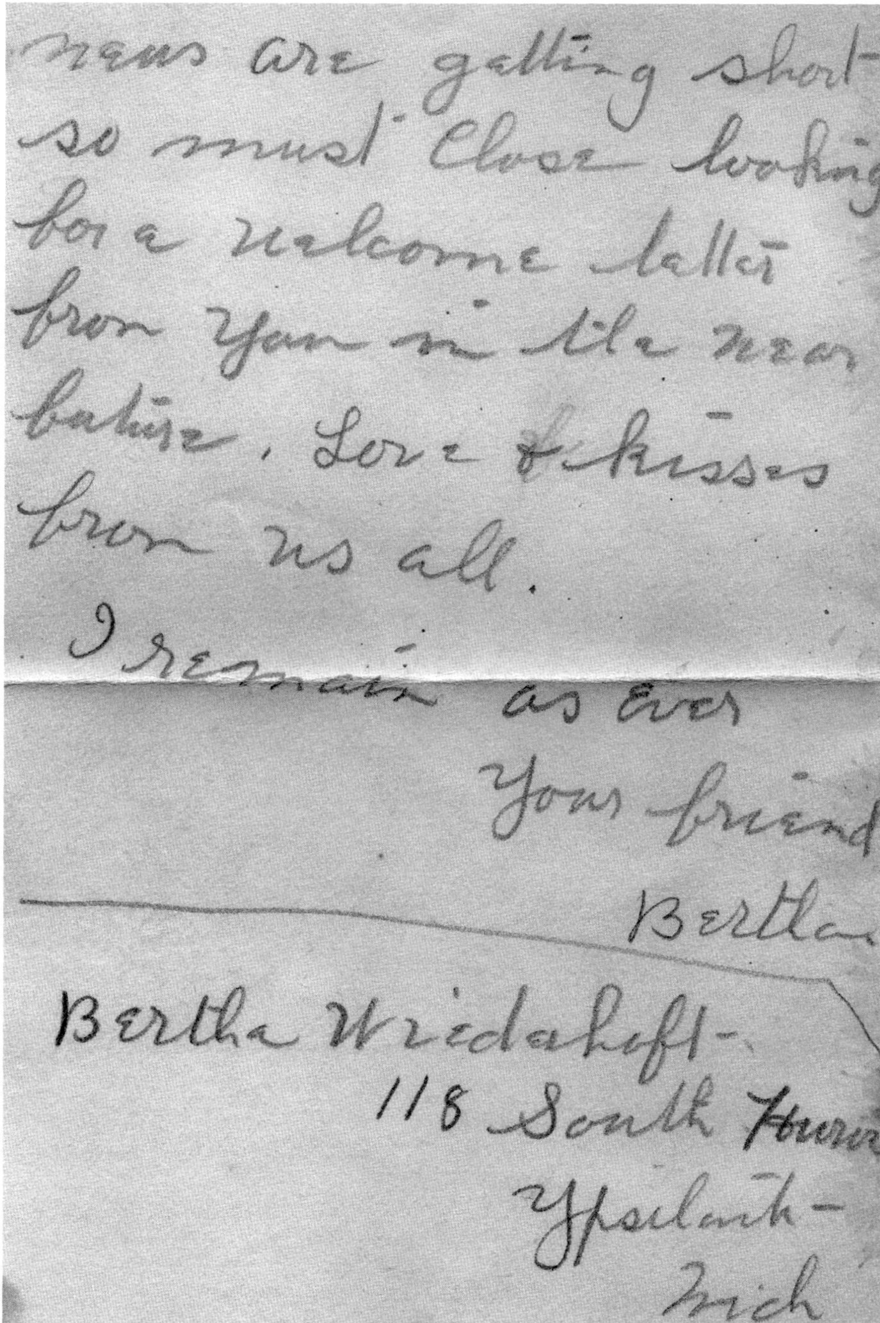
news are getting short
so must close looking
for a welcome letter
from you in the near
future. Love & kisses
from us all.
I remain as ever
Your friend
Bertha

Bertha Wiedahoft-
118 South Huron
Ypsilanti-
Mich

My dearest Emma—

Ypsilanti Mich

No 1 06

It is with pleasure I am answering your dear letter which I received yesterday + were more than pleased to hear from you. We are all well at the present writing + hope you are the same

Anna [Bertha's older sister] *and I are having our vacation this week + think It quite nice to have a rest for a week. But are having it quiet cold for our vacation. Although it is real pleasant + don't mind the cold. We went to Ann Arbor Tuesday to Ida's + had a very pleasant time had much fun with the baby. + yesterday we went out in the country to my Cousins on the Smith farm + spent the day there + had a nice time + today we stayed at home as I wanted to do some sewing.*

I made a waist [blouse] *for myself Monday + finished it today so you see I am quiet smart I wish you were here just this minute Mary is just acting up terrible I cant hardly wait till supper as mother is baking potato pan cakes I can taste them now you probably know how they taste so I won't have to tell you. Minnie* [Bertha's younger sister] *+ I did not go to Dearborn Sunday as the weather was very unpleasant + thought it best to stay at home I went to Church in the morning + the wind all most blew my head off. You probably wont be able to read this letter as the boys & Anne are bothering me so I can hardly write. Say Emma I have just got through with my supper + the Pototas Pan Cakes were fine + ate so much that I can hardly write*

You wrote about having a mother with five children + we think they must be Bunnies But perhaps the boys may be mistaken. We looked for your Father + Mother last Sunday + thought they would come But Mother thought they wouldn't come as it was so terrible windy + quiet cold + hope they can come Sunday. Emma two Doctors died here last week Dr. Mc. Andrew + Dr. Fraser was our family doctor both died. + Dr. Willcoxon is not expected to live as he has quick Consumption Well Emma my news are getting short so must close looking for a welcome letter from you in the near future. Love + kisses from us all.

I remain as ever

Your friend

Bertha

Bertha Wiederhoft

118 South Huron Ypsilanti

Mich

[Back of envelope stamped with] *CANTON / N/ 2 / MICH.*
[Front of envelope:] *Miss Emma King* [?]
Canton
Wayne Co.
Michigan
R.F.D. #1.

Though probably one of the poorer people in Ypsilanti in 1906, lacking even a father, working a difficult menial job and likely coming from a financially straitened home, Bertha sounds ebullient, loving and outgoing. She teasingly boasts to Emma about her completed waist, seems concerned about the death of her family doctor and had fun on her simple outing of a trip to her cousin's farm.

Bertha's good qualities were recognized by Herman Kruger. They married two years after Bertha wrote this letter.

Bertha and Herman celebrated their golden anniversary on July 22, 1958, with their son Frederick and daughters Rosena and Carol.

Bertha came close to celebrating her sixtieth anniversary with Herman. She died in the spring of 1968.

She is buried at Denton Cemetery.

Elijah Pilcher: Itinerant Methodist Preacher

Slimy logs shifting along the bank of Jackson's swollen Grand River trapped the horse's hock. But the animal's owner didn't curse. That would have been unseemly for the first itinerant Methodist preacher on the 1830 frontier Washtenaw circuit. Elijah Pilcher freed his horse's leg. He rode into the October-chilled water. Unexpectedly deep, it lapped over his thighs and into the leather saddlebags that held his Bible, his edition of Shakespeare and his only change of clothes. The horse struggled up the bank…and then sank into a marsh. "Stripping up to my sleeves," Elijah recalled later, "I thrust my hand into the mire and raised his feet and placed them upon new turf." Muddy and cold, he started for Ann Arbor at sundown with ten cents in his pocket.

Michigan was also new turf for the twenty-year-old blue-eyed boy, whose cast-iron stamina and vinegary humor would raise him from boyhood on a small Ohio pioneer farm to Michigan's state legislature in an era when half of all circuit preachers died, exhausted, before age thirty.

A vast, martial, Methodist itinerant minister campaign followed the ongoing westward settler migration in the early nineteenth century. Twenty-four ministers in 1776 increased to almost three thousand in Elijah's early career, due in part to the Methodist leadership's lackadaisical "entrance exam." It purportedly consisted of only four questions: 1. Is this man truly converted? 2. Does he know and keep our rules? 3. Can he preach acceptably? 4. Has he a horse?

Unlike other denominations more strongly tied to established church buildings, the itinerant Methodists gained frontier converts by personally visiting farm-bound settlers and preaching a populist doctrine of universal salvation and instantaneous conversion as a dramatic personal experience, as popularized at "camp meeting" revivals. Headed by bishops, the organization was subdivided into regional territories stretching over most of the nation. Each territory contained several districts. Elijah's district's woolliest stop was the rowdy frontier town of Jackson.

When Jackson was selected in 1839 for the state prison site, locals joked that Michigan should instead simply wall in the town to keep its residents captive. There, in "the bar-room of a log tavern, with the bottles staring me in the face," lifelong teetotaler Elijah preached one of his first Michigan sermons.

Settled only six years earlier, Ann Arbor lynchpinned Elijah's four-hundred-mile route. He preached twenty-eight times every four weeks, with days of two or more sermons alternating with days of horseback travel between Ann Arbor, Marshall, Coldwater, Clinton, Tecumseh, Adrian, Manchester and Saline.

The sparsely settled region had few roads. Elijah followed Indian trails or crossed marshes, oak openings and forests, spending four days near Marshall blazing trees with an axe from horseback to mark his way back. For days afterward, his right arm was crippled.

Circuit-riding preachers usually slept at the log cabins of the settlers they visited, preaching for bed and board. "The mansion was surrounded by a rail fence, in such a condition that it allowed the pigs to have free access to the yard, and…to the parlor," Elijah said of one cabin. "Besides them there were two or three dogs, which were commoners in the house, interspersed with some chickens and children." He spent that night in bug-infested bedding, wedged among children. "These are only some of the pleasures that go to make up the woof of an itinerant Methodist preacher's life, and tend to give spice and romance to it."

It may have additionally galled him to reflect that all of his listeners likely were better off, even the local farms' hired hands, who earned up to $1.00 a day. Millwrights earned $1.21, printers and blacksmiths $1.25, masons $1.26 and carpenters up to $1.50. For Elijah's year's worth of ministering to sometimes hostile settlers, traveling through snowstorms and even misplacing his horse near Coldwater, he received $87.00. Given his daily workload and assuming two weeks off for holidays, his wage equals $0.25 a day, equivalent today to $5.00. "Who, not moved by the Holy Ghost to the work of the ministry, would undertake it?" Elijah later wondered. "Long and fatiguing rides were to be performed on horseback; storms were to be breasted; rivers and smaller streams were to be forded and swum; lodgings were to be found in rude log cabins, and sometimes with ruder people."

This Job-like list of hardships temporarily ended when Elijah obtained a coveted ministerial "station" in Ann Arbor in 1837. During other, later stints in the city, he served as a U-M regent from 1845 to 1851 and earned a medical degree from U-M in 1859, though he never practiced. But the Methodists kept their ministers moving. Elijah was sent on routes from Kalamazoo to Canada and served as presiding elder in Monroe, Adrian, Port Huron, Detroit and Ontario. He founded thirteen churches, in Detroit (three), Manchester, Dexter, Chelsea, Saline, Jackson, Grass Lake, Marshall, Coldwater, Ingham and Hastings. In between, he earned a law degree, helped found Albion College, bought land in Jackson for a farm where he "evolved vegetables" and wrote editorials for the *Kalamazoo Gazette* boosting agricultural schools, which helped spur the legislature's establishment of the Michigan Agricultural College, now MSU.

Each year, the Methodists gave a one-year break to "superannuated, or worn-out preachers." Elijah requested this sabbatical in 1836 after the first of his three marriages and again in 1879 to write his relentlessly detailed *Protestantism in Michigan: Being a Special History of the Methodist Episcopal Church and Incidentally of Other Denominations.* The book presents a biographical inventory of Michigan ministers in dignified, floral prose—with one exception. Of the Grand Rapids church, he says, "This whole valley only returned twenty-seven members in 1836. The next year there was no report, owing to circumstances over which we prefer to draw a veil."

This referred to Frederick Seaborn, who'd been run out of town for lewd behavior, heaved onto a gaunt horse with a bundle of straw dressed in women's clothes tied behind him. Seaborn was the exception to Michigan's minister corps, who helped raise Methodism to such a force that in 1868 Ulysses S. Grant remarked that there were three great parties in the United States—the Republican, the Democratic and the Methodist Church.

In old age, Elijah suffered a stroke that crippled his right arm, so he learned to write with his left. When he sent his recollections to the Pioneer Society of Michigan, he didn't mention the churches he'd founded or his roles as presiding elder. Nor did he mention his degrees, honors or difficulties.

He dwelt instead on his long-ago green years as a young itinerant in Michigan. Then, a day's accomplishment consisted of preaching to an audience of two, composing a sermon on horseback over lonely miles or freeing a horse's foot in an October sunset.

Part II

BAD TIMES

LOCAVORES IN 1930S YPSILANTI

Before locavorism became fashionable for those rich enough to choose their foods, it was the default position of the poor. In 1932, property owners all over Ypsilanti responded to an appeal by local social worker Inez Graves and donated vacant lots for community food gardens.

Conditions were desperate. The American Legion bought surplus army uniforms to give to the poor for everyday clothing. The city accepted tons of government flour—several times. Ypsilanti also allowed the cutting of trees by unemployed men "who can burn wood in their home stoves," noted the *Ypsilanti Daily Press*.

As city trees came down, tomatoes, peppers and beans were coming up. Ypsilanti landowners responded to the *Press*'s call for tillable ground, but demand outstripped supply. "Calls for Garden Plots Exceed Number Listed," noted an April 1, 1932 *Ypsilanti Daily Press* headline. The paper asked for more lots within the city limits, since many families didn't have a car.

Five days later, the *Press* repeated, "More Lots for Gardens Needed to Meet Demand," though over one hundred lots were already being tilled. "Guy Comstock has listed lot 165, Ainsworth Park, and Mrs. Philip Santure, 413 Ferris St., has three lots on Miles St., next to Wolf's which are available."

As the new sprouts poked up on the plots, the police issued a stern warning "that owners of chickens must keep them confined, or face possible arrest and conviction on charges of maintaining a nuisance," according to the April 7, 1932 *Press*. The paper quoted Officer Ernest Maddux: "Gardens and bulbs are beginning to come up, and chickens are doing damage. Several people have been warned, but if the warning is not heeded, action will follow."

Throughout that April, property owners continued to donate lots, and demand continued to exceed available land. The sight of city plows digging vacant lots and residents hoeing and planting them became commonplace. Need grew so great that at least one resident offered her own backyard: "Mrs. M.J. Davis, 710 W. Michigan Ave., has offered the use of the lot at the rear of her home," said the April 11, 1932 *Press*.

The civic spirit evident in such generosity reappeared in the fall, when groups all over town volunteered help to can produce. Church, school and neighborhood groups canned bushels of fruits and vegetables and crushed a large crop of sorghum for a sugar substitute. The sorghum had been grown in the schoolyard of Harriet School (now Perry Child Development Center).

Hundreds of Ypsilantians opened jars of peaches, beans and tomatoes well into the winter. For some people, on some nights, it was the only bowl of food on the table.

Many families had shortages in Depression-era Ypsilanti. But as the gardening effort showed, one thing the town didn't lack was generosity among neighbors.

YPSILANTI'S FIRST SUPERMARKET

Most people think of the invention of supermarkets as simply a natural effect of increasing modernity in the 1950s.

In Ypsilanti, one supermarket arose much earlier, and for a different reason.

In 1940s Ypsilanti, ration books were used to mete out food. Fuel was in short supply. City scrap rubber drives were in full swing, and it was difficult, if not impossible, to get new tires for your car. People drove less and tried to conserve their cars until better times. Although many of the small grocers delivered to your door, the delivery system was better suited to stay-at-home moms, not households in which the husband was serving overseas and the wife was out doing war work. For wartime motorists shopping after work, the city's longtime system of scattered, separate meat markets, poultry markets and small grocers was becoming difficult and costly to navigate.

The July 9, 1942 *Ypsilanti Daily Press* reported that "a $75,000 streamlined food department store, representing A&P Tea Company's latest contribution to war-forced 'one-stop shopping,' where complete food requirements are obtainable under one roof, was opened here today at Michigan Ave. and Grove St." Four A&Ps already existed in Ypsilanti. These were small "economy" stores not much bigger than the existing traditional grocers. The Michigan and Grove store was new and represented a nationwide scale.

The paper continued:

> *In announcing the store opening, James A. O'Donnell, vice-president in charge of the company's Detroit unit, said the new red and buff colored brick structure is the "most modern food establishment in the country which features more and larger 'stores within stores' than any other retail outlet."*

"The store replaced A&P's first super market in its Detroit unit, which was opened three blocks west at 23 Michigan Ave. in February, 1937," the paper noted. This was one of the four small "economy" stores. The use of the word "super" is debatable, since the parking lot had spaces for only fourteen cars.

The new store's lot boasted an eighty-car parking lot and the novelty of fluorescent lighting. Six checkout lanes served customers.

In comparison to the old store, the new one had "30 feet of meat and fish cases, 20 feet more than the other store; 36 feet of dairy boxes and cases, while the old store had only a 10-foot-long wall box…and a 65-foot tile-covered fruit and produce rack equipped with the latest slanting back-mirror." In addition, the chain's economies of scale allowed it to undercut local grocers in price, another appealing factor for rationed wartime budgets.

A&P executives from Detroit, New York and Chicago attended the grand opening. As a first step toward Washtenaw County's modern big-box food

The advent of supermarkets led to the disappearance of small grocers around town, such as the Lamb-King grocery, seen here in 1928. *Courtesy of Ypsilanti Archives.*

stores, Ypsilanti's sparkling new A&P offered an appealing way to save scant wartime money and transportation resources.

THE SADNESS IN A DEPRESSION-ERA GROCERY RECEIPT

The pathos of the Depression still shows up today, seventy-odd years later. You can see it.

It could be a grandmother who keeps all of her kitchen cupboards, two hall cupboards and a fridge and freezer so stuffed with cans and packages of food that there isn't room for anything more, with the stuff in the back, untouched, perhaps ten years old.

It could be a grandfather who for Christmas gives a thirty-year-old granddaughter a worn and outdated thermos picnic set bought at a garage sale because it's "still good."

Or it could be a 1930 grocery receipt from the Ypsilanti Archives.

John G. Lamb's grocery, formerly Charles King's grocery, was possibly the longest-running one in Ypsilanti, lasting from 1840 to World War II. It was also one of the first to institute a cash system. But by the Depression, the store had gone back to running monthly tabs for its customers. The one on the next page is from P.R. Cleary.

Irish-born former penmanship teacher P.R. Cleary was the founder and president of Cleary College at this time; he would retire eight years later at eighty years of age. His wife was the president of the Ypsilanti chapter of the Daughters of the American Revolution (DAR) and a member of the Ladies Literary Club. The Clearys had four successful children: Charles, Marjorie, Ruth and Owen. The couple was active and prominent in Ypsilanti social doings. But in 1930, they apparently could not pay their grocery bill.

For the month of January, Cleary bought $25.92 in groceries. He already had a running tab of $156.64 ($2,000 in today's dollars), and the January foods brought his bill up to $182.56 ($2,300). A terse note from the grocer is written sideways on the bill: "A payment will be appreciated/J.G. Lamb & Son."

It was a grim time, even for college presidents. Here is a transcription for each January day:

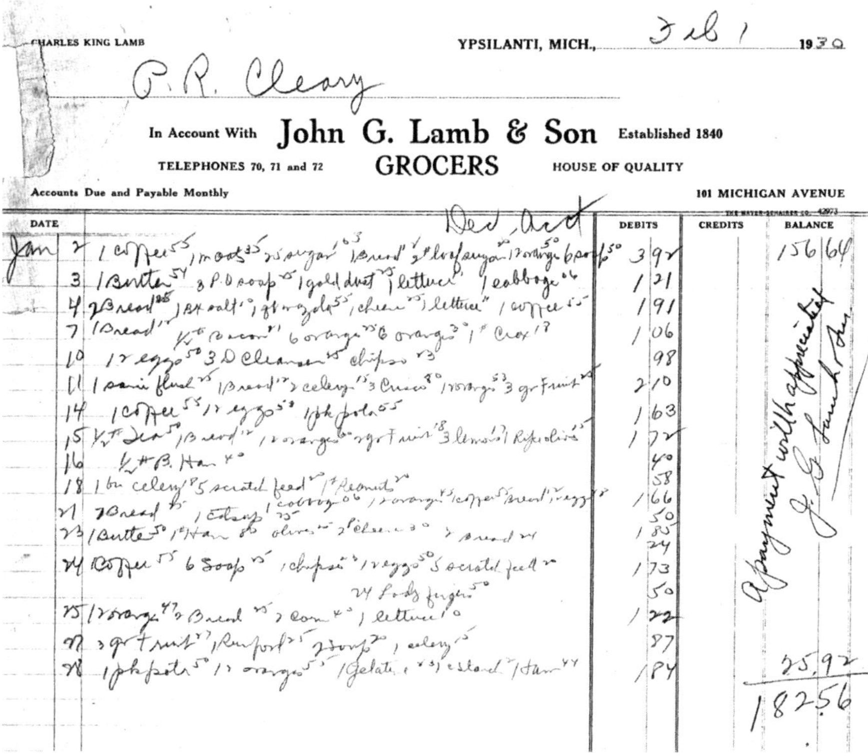

CHARLES KING LAMB

YPSILANTI, MICH., Feb 1 1930

P.R. Cleary

In Account With **John G. Lamb & Son** Established 1840

TELEPHONES 70, 71 and 72 **GROCERS** HOUSE OF QUALITY

Accounts Due and Payable Monthly

101 MICHIGAN AVENUE

DATE		DEBITS	CREDITS	BALANCE
Jan	2	3 92		156 64
	3	1 21		
	4	1 91		
	7	1 06		
	10	98		
	11	2 10		
	14	1 63		
	15	1 72		
	16	40		
	18	58		
	21	1 66		
	23	1 85		
	24	1 73		
	25	1 22		
	27	87		
	28	1 84		25 92
				182 56

A payment will be appreciated

J. G. Lamb & Son

In the age of small local grocers, one Cleary family member went food shopping about every other day. *Courtesy of Ypsilanti Archives.*

2 1 coffee, 1 lb. oats, 25 sugar, 1 bread, 2 lb. loaf sugar, 12 oranges, 6 soap

3 1 butter, 3 P.O. soap, 1 gold dust [scrubbing cleanser], *1 lettuce, 1 cabbage*

4 2 bread, 1 box salt, 1 qt. mazola, 1 cheese, 1 lettuce, 1 coffee

7 1 bread, 1/2 bacon, 6 oranges, 6 [more expensive] *oranges, 1 lb. rackers*

10 12 eggs, 3 D [Dutch] *Cleanser, chipso* [laundry soap flakes]

11 1 sani flush, 1 bread, 2 celery, 3 Crisco, 12 oranges, 3 grapefruit

14 1 coffee 12 eggs, 1 peck [quarter bushel] *potatoes*

5 1/2 lb. tea, 1 bread, 12 oranges, 2 grapefruits, 3 lemons, 1 ripe olives

16 1/2 lb. B. ham [?]

18 1 celery, 5 [lbs?] *scratch feed* [for chickens] *1 lb. peanuts*

21 2 bread, 1 catsup, 1 cabbage, 12 oranges, 1 coffee, bread [cheaper], *12 eggs*

23 1 butter 1 lb. ham, olives, 2 cheese, 2 bread
24 coffee 6 soap, 1 chipso, 12 eggs, 5 [lbs?] *scratch feed*
25 12 oranges, 2 bread, 2 corn [?] *1 lettuce*
27 3 grapefruit, 1 rumford [baking powder], *2 soup, 1 celery*
28 1 peck potatoes, 12 oranges, 1 gelatin, starch, ham

THE ANGEL OF THE DEPRESSION

Ypsilanti did not plunge into poverty in the fall of 1929.

The stock market crash was, for many, just a news item. The city's descent into the Depression was gradual. Retail trade began to decline by December 1929. Factories started to lay off workers. About two years after the crash, the Ypsilanti Savings Bank closed. More jobs disappeared. By the time 1932 arrived, children were staying home from school because of inadequate clothing.

There was no unemployment money or Social Security in 1932. However, the city was still in the end of an era of municipally provided services. It had its own gas plant, at Huron and Cross, and shutoffs for nonpayment were rare. Ypsilanti had its own water works, too, in the present-day Waterworks Park. The local companies were lenient toward their neighbors in the way more distant corporations might not have been. The mercy of these municipal utilities allowed many poor Ypsilantians a bit of breathing room in the early '30s, when conditions were becoming dire.

Another municipal resource was the official city social worker, a single woman who worked tirelessly for decades in the Depression and for years afterward to help her fellow Ypsilantians. Her name was Inez Graves.

If your family was one of the dozens of families in need in the "Dirty Thirties," Inez was the person who put several quarts of canned goods on your kitchen table—canned here in Ypsi—and gave you a pair of reconditioned shoes for your son. Although numerous local groups including the Red Cross and the American Legion also provided support, Inez was the single most prominent social relief worker during the Depression.

Born to a carpenter and a housewife in Wisconsin, Inez was the oldest child, with one younger sister, Edith. Inez came to Ypsilanti in 1920 at age twenty-seven. In 1921, she founded the Business and Professional Woman's Club. This charity group bought a painting to loan out around town, decorated vacant store windows with edifying pictures of the Roman Arch and other architectural paragons and bought birdseed. The birdseed was given to rural postmen to take out on their route and scatter on the snow.

Inez didn't start out as city social worker, though by 1925 she was organizing such charitable events as a community Christmas tree for local children, as well as projects with the BPW. She worked as a school attendance officer and lived in modest circumstances at 324 West Forest Avenue.

By 1930, howevwer, she had achieved her dream of becoming a municipal social worker. In this year, Inez worked to provide milk money to poor students at Woodruff School. She also coordinated relief efforts for a family whose house burned down. The family was given a new house rent-free (though the men had to help build a barn), as well as furniture and clothing.

In 1931, Inez used the *Ypsilanti Press* to call for clothes. Working with the *Press*, she organized a community garden program in which property owners donated over one hundred vacant lots to community members who planted vegetable gardens. She also helped coordinate canning projects in which church and community groups canned hundreds of quarts of local produce that Inez later distributed to the poor.

In 1932, Inez oversaw the distribution of federal "relief wheat." She reinstated the community gardening plan and was appointed to a mayoral relief committee to help organize the efforts of the numerous groups in town providing relief efforts. As the Depression wore on, Inez could often be found at the city's welfare office, at Michigan Avenue and River Street.

In 1935, President Roosevelt created the Social Security Act, which included unemployment relief. Inez continued to work for the remainder of the Depression and into World War II. Though she was now the official city services director, she still lived in modest surroundings as a renter on Cambridge Road.

In 1966, Inez was honored at a special banquet for her forty years of service to the city. The fancy dinner was a world removed from the cold houses she'd visited years ago, bringing socks and a patched shirt, and from the rundown shacks whose doors she'd knocked on, carrying a basket of canned beans and peaches.

Inez Graves worked long days for decades to fill the plates and clothe the backs of her Ypsilanti neighbors, before returning alone each night to her rented room. She died in 1975, almost ninety years old. It's only fitting that Ypsilanti's greatest example of selflessness, charity and love of one's fellow man was born, all those years ago in 1892, on a special day.

December 25.

NEEDLES, RAGS AND AN OLD PEACH TREE

From teacher Lois Prout's classroom "one can see a two room home made of packing case wood" with paper nailed on as a flimsy covering, "in which a large family is planning to spend the winter."

Inside the classroom, one ten-year-old girl carefully cuts along markings on a man's worn blue shirt to create three pieces. Another mends knee holes in a man's pair of woolen underwear. A third shows Miss Prout the half-yard of new red cloth that her dad had bought her. Combined with some other scraps, it would make enough for an apron.

In 1930, the fourth- and fifth-grade girls at Harriet School altered old, worn-out clothes into wearable ones that "will clothe children who otherwise might suffer from the severe weather. Stockings, silk, wool, or cotton, are being painstakingly mended…and even old underwear is being cut down to keep little boys and girls warm."

Not only were the children sewing usable garments that were going back into the community, but they were also doing it with style—they were hand-sewing on bias tape. This is the colored decorative strip seen around the edges of things like potholders and aprons. It is folded three times and is devilishly difficult to sew accurately by hand. No problem for these ten-year-olds.

The girls also picked peaches from a tree next to the school and made peach jam. They canned tomatoes, pears, pickles and grape and crab apple jelly. They made taffy apple refreshments for a school party. Oh, and they planned to redecorate the home ec's model dining room.

There was no stopping these Ypsi girls.

Miss Prout is one of Ypsi's unsung heroes of the Depression. With some needles, some worn-out clothing and an old peach tree, she taught two grades of girls how to create useful, warm and nourishing things to benefit the community around them.

Ypsilanti's Depression-Era Zoo

In 1937, "Miss Ypsi" the monkey, ponies, bears, foxes, a parrot, a collection of snakes and other animals lived in an improvised zoo in Tourist Park (now Waterworks Park). The animals came from western Michigan, Iowa, Florida, Canada and South America. Several were purchased with money raised by Ypsilanti schoolchildren.

"Two baboons will soon be installed in their quarters at the Tourist Park," said the April 21, 1937 *Ypsilanti Daily Press*. "Free will collections are to be taken among the school children...to furnish money to buy the animals."

"Within a week's time," the paper continued, "it is expected that the $75 will be raised by the children. That about covers the cost of both baboons."

The baboon cages stood in Tourist Park, a public campground just off Catherine Street in today's Waterworks Park. Families came from as far away as Virginia to park their trailers or pitch their tents in the park while they attended summer classes at the Normal School (EMU). It was an economical mode of life in a difficult time.

The park entrance featured the bronze statue of a woman. Once the top half of Ypsilanti's twelve-and-a-half-foot-high Starkweather Fountain, which stood outside the present-day city hall, the statue had been detached from the fountain in 1932. The graceful Hebe, goddess of Youth, gazed benevolently over the children running to the nearby zoo to see its latest additions.

"The plot thickens at the Ypsilanti Tourist Park zoo with the arrival of a second crow, donated by a Saline resident who read in the *Daily Press* that the camp's original bird had been sadly gored by a menagerie mate, the billy goat," noted the *Ypsilanti Daily Press* in an undated story.

Warming to his subject, the reporter continued:

> *Crows...have individual personalities—there's determination and a buoyant zest for life in the way Old Black Joe cocks his head; there's grim disillusionment and cynical aloofness in the jaded eye of Oscar. Joe is much given to chasing bantam chickens in the park, and Oscar, who no longer sees the world through the rosy haze of innocence, bides his time until Joe will receive his inevitable punishment for his carefree disregard of the chickens' cherished rights to the pursuit of life, liberty, and happiness. One day, gloats Oscar, Joe will learn that the little feathered beasties, for all of their empty-headedness, have a mind of their own.*

The bird collection included two parakeets, "Their shimmery blue and turquoise coats laced with black and white grace the menagerie with an air of aristocratic elegance," said the *Press*. "Their manners are impeccable, a lesson to the monkey if she were only quick to catch on to things of that sort. The parakeets, from South America, also lend a romantic note to the otherwise hard-headed, practical zoo inhabitants. They sit close together, spooning all day long and far, far into the night, oblivious to everyone else in the world."

The parakeets lived with Mac the parrot and several smaller birds in an improvised birdhouse. "One of the cleverest arrangements which Mrs. Flagg and her brother Mr. Welsh have contrived is the new bird house," said the June 30 *Press*.

> *It was formerly seen on Ypsilanti streets as a popcorn booth, but it is singularly well adapted for its present purpose. In a very neat and workmanlike manner, the open spaces on three sides have been fitted with solid blinds, which drop down and the fourth side has been outfitted with heavy canvas curtains which when unrolled make excellent protection against wind and cold.*

Two animals arrived from Canada. "Two brown bears, gift of Ypsilanti school children, are in Ypsilanti Tourist Park today," said the May 22 *Press*. "They are both a deep brown, weigh about ten pounds apiece, and are two months old."

One month later, the paper gave an update. "A surprising attachment has sprung up between the little bears and the little white dog; the dog is allowed in the cage to play with the bears at intervals…In the evening the bears are taken out on chains which run along a wire, and the place where they chase each other and tramp back and forth is worn bare."

Foxes from Iowa joined the zoo. "Two red foxes two months old…scamper about their cage and already seem a little less wild than on their arrival," said the May 22 *Press*. "They are pretty little things with light brown eyes looking directly at visitors and with neat black legs that are carrying them forward and back in the cage playing at present with a tin can."

The collection included a king snake, several garter snakes and blue racers sharing quarters with a big frog. "How to help the snakes shed their skin was somewhat of a problem until Mr. Welsh lined the floors of their cages with small gravel," said the June 30 *Press*. "Several have shed their skins this week. A corn or red rat snake, coming from Florida, is very handsome since shedding his old skin Monday and is a distinct red in parts."

At the end of June, two ponies appeared. "Both are jet black," said the June 30 *Press*. "Joe is distinguished from Lucky in having one white spot. They have bridles and saddles and look lively even when standing at rest occasionally under the trees with children clustered about them."

Though the zoo's animal housing and care were not up to modern standards, the little homemade zoo brought fun and diversion to Ypsilanti children and families in a difficult time. It was one symbol of the resourcefulness and grit of Ypsi residents who, though pressured by poverty and want, created something beautiful.

1932 Harvest Festival

Some children in Depression-era Ypsilanti could not attend school because they didn't have enough pieces of clothing.

Others attended barefoot, and one newspaper story of the era advised teachers to make sure that the barefoot students weren't teased by the students who were lucky enough to have shoes.

Another story described an Ypsilanti teacher asking why one of her students hadn't brought a lunch. The little girl replied, "It's my sister's day to eat."

In the gray year of 1932, the city was receiving shipments of federal flour as food aid to the poor. City council was trying to enforce a five-day workweek, instead of six, for city employees so that more men could have work. Local church and community groups were canning the summer's produce for distribution to the poor. The song "Brother, Can You Spare a Dime" had just been published the year before. But in the fall of 1932, Ypsilanti displayed gumption and energy by organizing a Harvest Festival.

"Mardi Gras! Gay crowds forgetting care and the realities of this world!" said the September 27 *Ypsilanti Daily Press*. "Carnival! Lights, music, color, dancing girls, and the mystery that hides behind canvas tents. Harvest Festival! Abundance of field and orchard in rich autumn coloring as men and nature dress in new attire for a new season." Organized by the American Legion and held on a closed section of Michigan Avenue between Adams and Huron Streets, the festival also featured merchant booths, a car show, Shetland ponies, a Ferris wheel set up in front of the post office (now the downtown library), a carousel and a "chair plane" carnival ride nearby.

The festival offered fun to local children. "There will be tiny tots there who never went to school and whose heart beats have never quickened to the rollicking tunes of the merry go round," noted the *Press*. "What fun Dad will have holding them on the iron horses!" The carousel stood at Michigan Avenue and Washington Street.

"Older ones can venture onto the Ferris wheel, which they watched from the ground when they were 'too little' to get on it," the paper continued.

> *And all the dreams they have dreamed about that first ride will come true...* [t]*here will be the gradual rise to the top and the slow sinking to the ground the first turn round when one hardly dares to open his eyes. Then the second trip, when one's courage increases and one can by holding tightly to the guard rope, take a glance at the world below. Mother's face looks smilingly up from oh such a long way down, and one lets go the rope to grasp Daddy's comforting hand. But the third trip is exquisite! Then you can hear the music below, see the lights and gay costumes, and feel the shiver of surprise wriggle through your whole being! That first ride is worth the summer's anticipation.*

"The next step is the chair plane, where you have to sit alone and spin through the air at what seems to be an appalling rate," the paper continued. "The world comes and goes to your surprised vision in kaleidoscopic array. You can hardly swallow and the wind on your face makes you breathless. You have a detached feeling and then you begin to float in circles and finally your feet can again skip along the ground as the contrivance slows down for the end of the ride." The chair plane stood at Michigan Avenue and Adams Street.

The festival was a success. Ten thousand people attended its opening night, and an even larger crowd attended the next day. Bands from the city, Milan and Adrian performed, and local business owners mingled among the attendees in colorful costumes and masks, Mardi Gras–style.

No crimes were reported during the two-day festival, and late on Saturday night the clean-up crew swung into action with brooms and wagons so that, the *Press* noted, "Sunday morning found the business section as free of unpleasant reminders as if there had been no festival."

For two days, Ypsilanti kids had a chance to forget their troubles and escape into a magical world filled with lights and music, where the Ferris wheel lifted them high into the air and where Shetland ponies became, noted the *Press*, "race horses, plow horses, cavalry horses, and broncos to the boys and girls who ride them."

CASH FOR CLUNKERS IN 1938 MICHIGAN

The popular "Cash for Clunkers" program had a Depression-era predecessor, "National Used Car Exchange Week." Created by automakers in 1938, the promotion was meant to ease the glut of used cars clogging dealerships. Then, as now, people frightened by the economic climate were hanging on to their old cars, which stifled dealership turnover.

Edsel Ford, General Motors' William Knudsen and Chrysler's K.T. Keller met with President Roosevelt in January 1938. Afterward, Ford sales manager John Davis contacted Automobile Manufacturers Association president Alvan Macauley to say the plan was greenlighted. From Manhattan, Macauley announced that U.S. automakers would spend over $1 million to promote March 5–12, 1938, as "National Car Exchange Week." The plan included a one-week campaign of billboard, radio and newspaper ads promoting the exchange of one's old car for a newer used one.

"National Car Exchange Week" first appears in the February 28, 1938 *Ypsilanti Daily Press*, with the headline "Advertising to Break Auto Jam":

> *The American automobile industry moved as a unit for the first time in history today in an effort to beat the business recession with one of the greatest advertising campaigns of all time. The industry...announced Sunday that it will spend $1,250,000* [almost $19 million in 2009 money] *in a single week to break the used car jam that has been blamed for the collapse of the market for 1938 model cars.*

On March 1, another story appeared:

> *Edsel Ford, William Knudsen, and K.T. Keller today threw the weight of the motor industry's "big three" behind the $1,250,000 advertising campaign to end the business recession by breaking the jam of used cars in the stocks of dealers...Ford, a "second generation" man of a motor family that has been known for its independent action, spoke of the*

Ford tried to move inventory by advertising the sale as a chance to upgrade. *Courtesy of Ypsilanti Archives.*

industry as a whole, saying: "The one great contribution the automobile industry made to the nation in its efforts to throw off the last depression was its demonstration of courage in the face of adversity. That same fearlessness is evident today as a united industry moves forward to start the wheels rolling again."

By March 2, the Ypsilanti community had made plans. "Local Car Dealers Take Part in National Drive," read one *Press* headline. "Ypsilanti auto dealers meeting at the Huron Hotel Thursday unanimously agreed to cooperate with manufacturers and 46,000 other dealers throughout the United States in a campaign to break the used car jam and to aid in sound recovery from the current business recession." A parade was planned, and the *Press* printed a mayoral proclamation:

> *Whereas, a concerted movement to stimulate used car sales and pave the way for a resumption of automobile manufacturing and employment on a normal basis has been inaugurated by the American automobile industry, and*
>
> *Whereas, the business interests of Ypsilanti have pledged their enthusiastic cooperation to this campaign, and*
>
> *Whereas, the "Drive-A-Better-Car" movement will make an important contribution to motoring safety in Ypsilanti, now*
>
> *Therefore, I hereby proclaim the week of March 5 to 12 National Used Car Exchange Week and urge the cooperation of all citizens in insuring its success.*
>
> *Witness my Hand and Seal, Ray H. Burrell, Mayor.*

In the same paper, a cartoon titled "ANCHORS OR WINGS?" boosted the program. In the first panel, an antiquated old jalopy is dragging a ship's anchor. "Holy smoke, Myrt," says the driver. "What's got into this moss-grown tub? We're shovelin' out the price of a summer trip for gas, oil, and repairs!" In the next panel, a sleek new car appears. "Baby, what National Used Car Exchange Week did for us! More room—steel body—safety brakes—big tires—smooth engine. Looks like we're in the dough, but most of the dough is still in my pocket!"

Ypsi's E.G. Wiedman Auto Company, at 212 Pearl Street and 15 East Michigan, ran an ad touting used car bargains. Prices ranged from $275 for a Ford DeLuxe Tudor Sedan to $795 for a Lincoln-Zephyr Fordor Sedan (in 2009 dollars, $4,000 and $12,000, respectively).

On Saturday, the campaign's opening day, the city woke up to ice and snow. Nevertheless, the parade went on as planned, featuring the Girls' Drum and Bugle Corps and the Ypsilanti High School Band, along with a procession of some sample used cars, washed and polished, from dealerships across town. Despite the weather, the day was a success: $10,000 (about $151,000 in 2009) in Ypsi dealership sales was reported.

By Tuesday, "First reports indicated marked increases in the sales of used cars," said the *Press*. "H.H. Shuart, manager of the Detroit Auto Dealers Association said dealers had reported last week end's business as the best in six months and that sales showed increases of 100 to 300 per cent. He said similar reports had been received from dealers in other cities."

The Wednesday paper quoted John Lonskey, president of the Ypsi metalworking firm Central Specialty Company: "In Ypsilanti alone, this will directly affect six factories with increased orders, meaning more employment and more money circulating in the city."

The paper continued:

> *In illustration of this Mr. Lonskey explained that in the case of the Central Specialty Co. there has been a drop in employment of 365 workers since the peak employment of last year when 850 men and women were employed. The emergency purchase of used cars throughout the country will result in putting automobile factories and related industries in operation everywhere with, in some cases, a 60 per cent or greater increase in demand for parts and equipment, he estimated. Many of these parts are made in this city.*

By the end of the week, National Used Car Exchange Week was deemed a success. Fifty-five old cars had been turned in by those who purchased newer ones, and a total of $18,000 worth of newer used cars had been sold.

Ypsilanti dealers were so pleased with the results that they planned to petition the state to mount another sales campaign in the future, this time by declaring 1932 model year cars as "marginal." In the meantime, the fifty-five Ypsilanti drivers behind the wheels of their new used cars had done their part to help get the local economy moving again.

THE FLAPPER BOOTLEGGER

When Ypsilanti bootlegger Clara Richards saw a police car in her driveway on October 22, 1923, she was not in a welcoming mood.

Police had obtained a warrant earlier that day to search her home at 306 Monroe Avenue on Ypsilanti's south side. Chief of Police John Connors, Deputy Sheriff Dick Elliott and Officer Ernest Klavitter left the car and approached the house.

It was the Roaring Twenties, the Jazz Age popularized in the novels of F. Scott Fitzgerald, and Clara tried to style herself as one of the era's svelte young "jazz babies." She got her hair cut in a fashionable bob, and when her name hit the papers, she was called a flapper.

But it was "flapper," in quotes—Clara was forty years old, with a rap sheet. One year earlier, Clara had been staying with Byron Tanner, who lived at 28 North Huron, where he also ran a secondhand store. Her occupation was listed as Tanner's housekeeper.

But when police raided Tanner's home in July, they found evidence of bootlegging and arrested him. Police suspected that Clara was in on it but didn't have enough evidence to charge her. Luck was with her and she went free. She moved to the Monroe Street house, where she lived alone.

Now, one year later, with police approaching her front door, Clara was determined that her luck wouldn't run out. She grabbed a jug of moonshine and ran to the kitchen sink, where she upended the jug. *Glug, glug, glug*—the incriminating 'shine was almost gone! The clear liquid spiraled down the drain.

There was only one problem: Clara's sink wasn't connected to the water system. The pipe went through her kitchen wall, draining wastewater into her yard. And at the end of that pipe, Clara saw Officer Connors collecting the moonshine as she poured it out. She desperately threw water into the sink, but it was too late. Connors had over a quart of evidence.

Clara was locked in the city jail but posted bail of $2,000 and went free. Her trial was scheduled for December, two weeks before Christmas.

The December 17, 1923 *Daily Ypsilantian-Press* said, "Some difficulty is being encountered in obtaining a jury"—likely because the case had figured so prominently in the paper. Eventually jurors were found, and the trial began.

Clara was found guilty.

She went to the county jail to await sentencing. As the newspapers filled with ads featuring Santa Claus and last-minute gift ideas, Clara received her sentence five days before the holiday: six months to one year in the Detroit House of Corrections.

Clara's luck had drained away.

THAT A MIND GONE WRONG COULD NOT PROTECT

"Yes, I'll sign!" "Me too; it's a disgrace!"

A petition was circulating in Ypsilanti in the summer of 1918. It demanded the release of Ypsilanti Civil War veteran John Norton, who was spending his seventh decade alone, widowed and far from home, in Grand Rapids' Soldiers' Home.

"Sure, where do I sign?" "Hey, give me that pen."

The petition was successful. Prior to John's release, doctors examined him to make sure he was sane and able to live on his own. John passed the tests and was released. He returned to Ypsilanti. He had been given $1,200 ($17,000 in 2009), meant as a pension to support him for the rest of his life.

He spent it in five days.

John spent the first chunk of money in opening a hotel in an old building on Huron Street once used as a post office. He offered prospective customers a "vegetable dinner, side dishes included" for fifteen cents.

No one came to eat John's vegetable dinner. The hotel failed.

John still had some of his $1,200. He spent the last of it on a second business venture, a shop selling used furniture. John arranged the furniture in his store and opened for business. It was his last chance.

No one came. Where were the petitioners who, with their signatures, had ransomed John from his forlorn life in Grand Rapids? These apparently fair-weather friends had faded away.

The furniture store failed. Now John was out of money in an era without unemployment relief or Social Security. He was penniless. Homeless, he could not find one sympathetic person to take him in.

But he hadn't been forgotten after all. The city appointed a guardian to John, B.R. Burbank. Burbank arranged for John to return to the Soldiers' Home. John returned to Grand Rapids, and Burbank was relieved.

For whatever reason, John soon returned to Ypsilanti. Now his plight was severe. Burbank searched for someone to put up the old soldier in a spare room but failed. He arranged the only shelter he could think of—the county jail.

John slept in the jail and ate prison food. The pockets in his worn-out clothes were empty, and the underwear beneath them, if he had any, was ragged. Winter was coming on. Burbank sold off some of the secondhand furniture in John's failed shop and bought him a coat, a suit of clothes and some underwear.

Either John's conduct had called into question his sanity, or the city could not tolerate the spectacle of a homeless Civil War veteran living in the jail. "A movement is now on foot to have him again examined," said the October 31, 1918 *Ypsilanti Record*, "and pronounced insane and sent to the Pontiac asylum."

The paper concluded, "Poor old soldier! He served his country well, and now, overtaken by old age, with no friends, no home, and money that would have gone a long way to provide the comforts for his last remaining days lost in a pile of junk wished on him for the greed of the mighty dollar that a mind gone wrong could not protect."

THE 1925 DEATH OF WILLIAM MAGER

The six men in the woods bent over the shallow grave. In it lay a man buried face down. Hands gripped his old work coat and overalls and hauled him out. On the new-fallen snow amid the leaves and dirt that had covered him, the man stared unseeing into the bare November branches above as dusk fell.

Police Chief Connors turned to the handcuffed man. "Aren't you sorry? There is your father, the man who played with you when you were a boy, and you killed him."

"Aren't you sorry?" The man he spoke to didn't look threatening. At five foot, eight inches tall and 135 pounds, he had a medium frame, disheveled brown hair and, in a gaunt face, blank blue eyes. "Yes, in a way," he answered. "In a way, I'm not."

Officers took away Harold Mager, and the body of his father, Salem township farmer William Mager.

Born in 1868 to German-born stonecutter William Mager Sr. and his wife, Catherine, William Jr. was the baby of the family. He lived with his parents and older siblings, Kate and Henry, in Ann Arbor. Henry left home when he grew old enough to buy a farm.

In 1892, at age twenty-four, William married the twenty-one-year-old Angeline. Between 1895 and 1900, William bought a farm, with a mortgage, near his brother Henry. He and Angeline had a baby, Ruth, in 1899. Henry had daughters as well, Laura and Viola, who attended the Salem Stone School.

By 1910, the forty-two-year-old William Jr. had paid off his mortgage. Eight years later, William owned two large farms and had the modern convenience of a telephone in his home, number 2-F3. He and Angeline had three children, Ruth, twenty; Harold, nineteen; and Mary, sixteen.

As Harold approached adulthood, he asked his father to give him one of the farms. His father said no. Father and son argued and tension grew. Shouting, yelling and possibly more violent actions strained the family.

About 1922, Angeline took the children and left. One record from this year shows a listing for a "Mager, Angeline" as a resident in U-M's Psychopathic Hospital. She died in 1923, allegedly from suicide. At the time of her death, Harold worked as a driver in Ann Arbor. He rented rooms at 822 Dewey Avenue with his sister Mary, a telephone operator for the Michigan State Telephone Company. They lived a frugal life.

However, Harold sometimes returned to his father's farm to work. He continued to plead for one of the farms. The two men usually ended up quarreling. About the fall of 1924, Harold became a resident of St. Joe's Sanitarium, an institution for the mentally ill.

He didn't stay long. When he left, he went to Whitmore Lake to buy a shovel. He also obtained a .32 revolver. He returned to the farm on Sunday morning, November 8, 1925. Harold asked the hired man, Clifton Adams, where his father was. Adams replied, "In the barn with the sheep."

Adams heard two shots. He saw Harold drive his car to the back of the barn out of sight. Harold reappeared, sped past Adams, drove down the driveway and disappeared.

Adams alerted police. "Led by Undersheriff Dick Elliott a posse of farmers and sheriff's officers searched the neighborhood all day Sunday, but failed to find either the body of the elder Mager, or any trace of the son," said the November 9, 1925 *Daily Ypsilantian-Press*. The search continued Monday.

On Monday evening, police received a call from Annie Dexter Gray, who with her husband owned a farm just north of Ypsilanti. She said there was a car parked on the road outside their property with a man inside.

The November 10 *Daily Ypsilantian-Press* said, "Driving out to the Gray farm… the officers found the machine parked near a small woods. Mager was sitting huddled up in the front seat. When Officer Oltersdorf opened the door of the car and asked him his name he readily admitted he was Harold Mager."

Mager was taken to the county jail. "Questioned last night," said the paper, "he said he had been looking for work for days. He had driven until a flat tire compelled him to stop, and as it was night, he decided to stop and sleep in the car until morning."

"Mager wore a cowhide coat, was spattered with mud, haggard and hollow-eyed," noted the paper. "The officers who saw him believe that his mental condition is not feigned. His mind seemed to wander, and he talked incoherently of events which had transpired years ago."

The next day, officers told Mager to find the body. Harold led officers all over Salem Township, through Ypsilanti and Ann Arbor. An escape attempt was thwarted, and his memory seemed faulty until officers told him, late in the afternoon, that if he did not find the body, they would return him to his father's farm. An angry mob of neighbors had congregated there. Harold then said that the body was in Webster Township. The officers found the body in a Webster Township farmer's woods as night fell.

Harold's trial began on November 18. Judge Sample heard testimony from police officers, Henry Mager and Clifton Adams. Sample found Harold guilty. "Standing before the bar, cap in hand," said the November 19 Daily *Ypsilanti Press*, "stoic, uncomprehending, his expressionless blue eyes fixed on the judge's face, he heard sentence pronounced without a trace of emotion."

Sample had Harold examined by doctors, who "found him suffering from a mental disorder, testifying he was devoid of emotion, suffered illusions of prosecution, was incoherent, had no realization of the seriousness of his situation and no regret for what he had done," reported the November 19 paper. "Dr. Klingman testified that he was in nearly the same mental condition a year ago when he first examined him. At that time he was a patient at St. Joseph's sanitarium." On November 20, sheriff's officers took Harold to a different institution: the Ionia Hospital for the Criminally Insane. William's farms were sold. The family was shattered.

Half a century later, it was quietly reunited. Harold died in 1986. Some unknown family member decided that it was appropriate to reunite Harold with his mother and father. They lie at rest together in the Mager family plot at Ann Arbor's Forest Hill Cemetery.

The Murder of Carter Deatherage

Farmhand "Cap" Deatherage woke from a stupor. He blinked and squeezed his eyes shut a few times. The barn's hayloft was cold. Snow was falling outside the loading door.

Deatherage stretched and slowly sat up. Farm work was over for the season; he'd have to overwinter in Ypsilanti. As he shuffled to the hayloft ladder, his foot hit an empty whiskey bottle. It was the Friday after Thanksgiving 1932.

A few hours later, in a dingy Ypsilanti "dance hall," Deatherage "ate, drank, and danced during the afternoon hours," reported the December 1, 1932 *Ypsilanti Daily Press*. He "drank excessively and finally lost consciousness. He fell across a dirty bed in the living quarters of the dance hall, where he slept as [several people] shuffled about in their dances without benefit of music."

The next morning, at 8:15 a.m., Ypsilanti South Side resident William Jones headed for the well in the back of his yard to get water. He walked past his chicken pen and a few dead tomato stalks sticking out of the snow. What he found at his well led to an investigation and trial that dominated city news for almost two weeks and caused an uproar in Jones's neighborhood, called "the Hill."

In an area roughly enclosed by Hamilton, Michigan Avenue and the modern-day I-94 stood streets of small homes alternating with run-down houses serving as blind pigs and so-called dance halls. The neighborhood had a tense mixture of struggling poor residents and a shifting population of drifters and criminals who preyed on their more settled neighbors.

Jones's "chicken yard has been robbed, on several occasions attempts have been made to enter his house; everything has to be kept under lock and key," read the December 1 *Ypsilanti Daily Press*. "'The Hill' is getting to be a place where respectable residents are obliged to carry arms. Three times in the last two years Mr. Jones has shot into the air to frighten away intruders."

This morning was far worse. Jones found a dying man at the well. His body lay on blood-soaked snow. Tire tracks led from the road to the well and back. The man's overcoat was torn up the back seam, and his collar, shirt and pants were ripped. As Jones approached, the man groaned. "By marks easily distinguishable, it is certain that the man was slashed at the spot where he was found," reported the November 26 *Press*. "He had been fiendishly attacked and a portion of his flesh was found 10 feet from the body." Jones called the police. The man was taken to Beyer Hospital with bruises and lacerations, a possible broken skull, broken neck and jaw and severe loss of blood. There he died.

During a search of the man's clothing, officers found the title and keys to an old Model T. The title indicated the car had been transferred to Carter Deatherage from Ed Wagner in Dundee. Police Chief Ralph Southard

A car theft may have motivated Deatherage's death. *Courtesy of Ypsilanti Archives.*

contacted Wagner and found that Wagner had bought the car from Glen Evert, who in turn had bought it from Mr. Sedimier. A clue came when an acquaintance of Sedimier's told police that a man matching the victim's description had worked for Milan-area farmer William Woolsey. Police found that Woolsey's son's employee, farm laborer Charles Garner, had seen the car's owner two days earlier.

Police arranged for Garner to view the body, which was undergoing an autopsy in Ann Arbor at the University Hospital. Garner confirmed that the body was that of Carter Deatherage. Garner told police that he had seen Deatherage on Thanksgiving Day, visibly drunk and complaining that he'd been beaten by a woman. Deatherage apparently had no local relatives with whom to spend the holiday. He slept in John Woolsey's barn on Thanksgiving night, said Garner, and disappeared some time on Friday.

Police learned that on Friday Deatherage had driven to Ypsilanti and returned to John Woolsey's farm with Hill resident O.D. Hall. At the farm, they collected Deatherage's clothing and the run-down trailer he had lived in, which Deatherage gave to Hall. Deatherage had arranged to overwinter in Ypsilanti in a shack on the Hill's Watling Street. Returning to Ypsilanti, Deatherage dropped off Hall. He bought some meat and headed for an abandoned house that now served as a dance hall at First and Jefferson. Already drunk, he wanted a "feed" and more liquor.

On the afternoon of the discovery of Deatherage's body, police took Hall in for questioning along with three other Hill residents: a white woman, Ellen Harvey, and African Americans Tom Britten and Frank Powell. Powell lived near and used to own the dance hall where Deatherage spent Friday afternoon. Recently released from the Detroit House of Correction for a liquor violation, Harvey was described by Police Chief Ralph Southard as Powell's housekeeper. Hall was released on Saturday afternoon, but the other suspects remained in custody over the weekend.

By Monday, November 28, after questioning the suspects, police learned that Deatherage had spent Friday afternoon in the dance hall. He was with Britten, Tom Kersey, Ed Talbert and Talbert's half brother Carey Hunt, also known as Casey Baylis, who was the current owner of the dance hall. Baylis had been released from the county jail on Thanksgiving after serving ten days for disorderly conduct. The men told police that Deatherage had passed out drunk, slept for most of the afternoon and had left at 5:00 p.m. Britten and Powell insisted that Ellen Harvey had not been there.

By now, police had found that Deatherage was a former army private in the 125th Infantry. He had entered the army in 1918 and was honorably discharged one year later after fighting in France. Police also found that Deatherage had a brother, Arthur, living on Terminal Avenue in Detroit. Arthur traveled to Ypsilanti for questioning. He disagreed with the police's theory that the crime was due to jealousy over a woman. Before returning to Detroit, Arthur said, according to the Monday, November 28 *Press*, that "his brother had shown no interest in women since he became involved with one accused of burning his home in Virginia."

On Monday afternoon, Deatherage was buried in Highland Cemetery. "There will be no mourners as the brother from Detroit is destitute and unable to finance a second trip to Ypsilanti," said the *Press*. "The expense of the funeral is taken from the county fund for soldier's burial. Brief rites will be conducted at the grave and there will be no pallbearers."

On Tuesday, November 29, the police again questioned Powell, Britten and Harvey. They also brought into custody and questioned Casey Baylis. "Their stories did not coincide and all repeatedly were trapped in lies," reported the

Tuesday, November 29, *Press*, "but up to a late hour this afternoon, officers had been unable to obtain an admission of guilt."

Contrary to Britten and Powell's earlier testimony, Ellen Harvey said that she had indeed been at the dance hall but left at 5:45 p.m. She said that Deatherage had been there. Britten, late on Monday, amended his story to say that Deatherage had been at the hall until 7:00 p.m. instead of 5:00 p.m. On Tuesday, he changed his story again to say that Deatherage had been there until some time between 10:00 p.m. and midnight. Britten was grilled throughout Tuesday by police officers and prosecutor A.J. Rapp. Officers also combed the crime scene. "Deatherage was not killed, officers are certain, on the Jones property. Automobile tracks near the pump house, and blood at the roadside, indicate he was brought there after the first attack had been made," noted the Tuesday, November 29 *Press*. "If he was killed in the [dance hall], it had been well cleaned up before officers arrived…Robbery is now considered the likely motive. Deatherage had money and had been spending it for liquor during the day. Police believe the gruesome lacerations about his abdomen may have been an afterthought, in an effort to send investigators off on a false clue."

On the morning of Wednesday, November 30, Britten confessed to murder. His confession detailed the last night of Deatherage's life. Britten said that he, Baylis and Deatherage had been in the dance hall late into the evening. Baylis urged Britten to rob Deatherage. But robbery wasn't the motive for the attack, claimed Britten. It was because Deatherage had flung a racial epithet at "the men of the race he had been taught to command at his home in the South," reported the December 1 *Press*.

Britten said Deatherage left the dance hall about midnight. As Britten followed him down the steps, he picked up a cudgel about three feet long. Britten said he followed Deatherage to the well and struck him twice, once on his head with the cudgel and once with his hand. "It is the opinion of Prosecuting Attorney Rapp that Britten, who is known to have a violent temper, struck Deatherage more than twice," read the Wednesday, November 30 *Press*. "Officers describe Britten as of a 'mean' disposition and recalled that on one occasion he had bitten a piece out of the arm of his wife, Edith. He has been arrested for desertion of her and their children and for disorderliness, but has not previously been implicated in a major crime. He has lived in Ypsilanti practically all his life."

On Wednesday, after signing his confession, Britten was taken to court. Pleading guilty, he was sentenced to life imprisonment in a Marquette prison. Baylis, who with Britten was jointly charged with the murder, pleaded not guilty. He headed to trial.

Baylis's Ann Arbor attorney, Louis Burke, told Ann Arbor's Judge Sample that the law allowed for a ten-day waiting period before the trial and that he needed time to prepare a defense. "Judge Sample stated that he was absolutely not in sympathy with delays and that it was his policy to mete out swift, sure justice," reported the Thursday, December 1 *Press*, "but because of the legal technicalities cited by Baylis' attorney, he allowed him until Saturday morning to determine at what time the case should be heard." Ellen Harvey was to be a witness. She did not face charges but did not make a favorable impression. The Thursday *Press* reported that "arrangements are being made to keep her from remaining in Ypsilanti."

Thursday's paper also contained an article headlined "Colored People of City Want 'The Law' to Clean Drifters Out of 'The Hill.'"

The article attributed trouble on the Hill as due to transient residents "asking no questions, giving and taking what they have or can find or steal in the way of food or clothing…Mr. Jones hopes the [murder, an] outgrowth of moonshine whiskey and disreputable mingling of the races, will bring about the needed reform. The respectable Ypsilanti colored people have had enough."

Two days later, the paper published a plea from Hill residents for Ypsilanti police to clean up the area. Chief of Police Ralph Southard agreed to monitor the neighborhood and responded by asking residents to watch their neighborhoods and inform police of suspicious characters. Three days later, Bertha Robinson was banned from the city and sent home to Flint after creating a disturbance at another dance hall. The watchfulness continued. The December 30 *Press* reported that police were patrolling the Hill and questioning strangers to make sure that they had legitimate business there.

On Monday morning, December 12, five witnesses testified in the Baylis trial. First was farmhand William Garner. He described his identification of the slain man and speculated as to how much money Deatherage had on his person. After Garner, Dr. F.B. Williamson described being called to Beyer Hospital to tend to the dying man. Next was Dr. E.C. Ganzhorn, Ann Arbor coroner. He corroborated Williamson's description of the injuries, described the autopsy procedure and gave as cause of death concussion of the brain and loss of blood.

Next on the witness stand came two officers, Coy Rankin and Ernest Maddux. The men described the scene where they'd found Deatherage and called an ambulance.

Shortly before noon, testimony was given by Tom Kersey, who lived in Casey Baylis's dance hall. He said Deatherage asked Hall for help in moving his trailer to Ypsilanti. Kersey said that he ended up going as well, along with

Britten, Baylis and Talbert, to the spot where the trailer had been left by the side of the road. Later, at the dance hall, Kersey testified that he had been called, by a person and for a reason he didn't name, into the rear section of the hall where Baylis had living quarters at about 10:30 or 11:00 p.m. He denied that he went there for liquor. Ellen Harvey followed him on the witness stand and testified that she had been at the dance hall and had two drinks while there.

The following morning, Tuesday December 13, Sheriff Jacob Andres offered testimony about a new confession that Britten had given the day before. The officer said Britten claimed that Baylis had helped Britten commit the crime. Prior to this claim, Baylis had been regarded only as an accessory. Andres reported that Britten confessed that both he and Baylis had pursued Deatherage. Baylis, said Britten, had a broken axe handle and he himself had a club; they had killed Deatherage together. According to Britten, Baylis then gave his knife to Britten and told him to disfigure the body. Baylis stole thirty-eight dollars from the body and gave Britten three dollars. Britten threw his club into the night. The two returned to the dance hall, where Baylis hid the axe handle under some potatoes and apples in a bin. They talked over the crime for three hours, agreed to keep quiet and went to sleep.

Britten next took the stand. He described the movements of all the people who had been at the dance hall Friday night. Other witnesses on Tuesday included George Randall and William Dailey, who were two deputies of Sheriff Andres; William Woolsey; Justice Jay Payne, who had first examined Baylis; and Chief of Police Ralph Southard, who said he had found Baylis's stick hidden in the dance hall.

With testimony concluded, after closing arguments the case went to the jury on Thursday, December 15. "It was decided not to force the jury to remain in the courthouse overnight," said the December 16 *Ypsilanti Daily Press*, "when it was discovered that beds kept in the building for that purpose were coated with nearly an inch of dust." Twenty-four hours later, the jury returned a verdict: not guilty.

The sad and sordid case was apparently over, but questions remain.

Why did Baylis and Britten insist that Ellen Harvey was not at the dance hall on the Friday Deatherage was there, although she herself said she was?

Why were there tire tracks leading to the well house and blood on the snow some distance from the well house, when Britten said he had been "following Deatherage [on foot] to the vacant lot where the well is located, [and] struck him"? The November 26 *Press* had reported, "It is evident by tracks that Deatherage was not killed near the spot where he was found… he had been apparently carried from a [car] to the side of the small well house." William Jones reported hearing a car "pass his house, turn the corner, and stop" between 4:30 and 5:00 a.m. on Saturday morning but didn't bother to investigate.

Why did police not search Deatherage's Model T? Where was the car? Although Deatherage had a set of keys on his person, suggesting that without them no one could drive his car, it was not only possible but also easy to hotwire Model Ts, or, for the older models, jury-rig a substitute key. When Deatherage came to town on Friday, with money and presumably a car, did the impoverished criminals on the Hill view him as easy pickings for car and bankroll theft?

Deatherage's existence was grim, lonely and short. It must be hoped that, in death, after his hardscrabble life, he at last found peace.

DOG TAGS FOR YPSILANTIANS

"If an atomic bomb drops (you can tell it by a sudden and great increase in light), drop wherever you are with your back to the light," instructed the December 8, 1950 *Ypsilanti Daily Press*. "Curl up to cover your bare arms, hands, neck, and face. Stay curled up 10 seconds. Then go to the nearest shelter to avoid flying glass and other objects blown about by the blast."

Fearing such an attack, in 1950 the Michigan Civil Defense commission picked four Michigan cities to test a pilot program that would issue every resident dog tags listing their blood type. The idea was to create a "mobile city-wide blood bank" in case of disaster. The state chose Ypsilanti as a representative residential-industrial town. It also chose Alma as a typical rural town, Birmingham as a residential center and Jackson for a county-wide program. If all went well, the state planned to roll out a statewide blood-typing program.

"The idea of mass blood typing in Michigan originated with the state commission as a civilian defense measure," noted the November 11, 1950 *Ypsilanti Daily Press*. "In the event of an atomic disaster or other highly destructive catastrophe, pre-knowledge of necessary blood types and the availability of supply would expedite the treatment of the injured. It was pointed out that such knowledge and supply would have greatly reduced the death rate resulting from atomic bomb blasts at Hiroshima and Nagasaki."

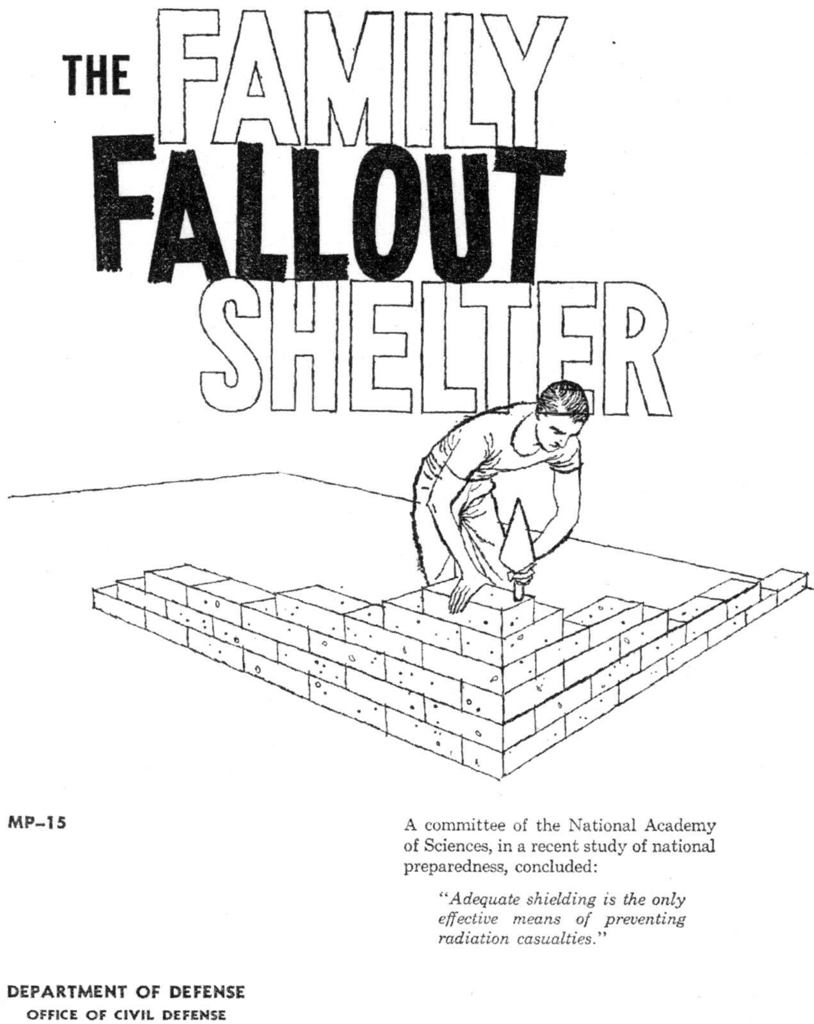

The cover of a detailed instruction manual for building a backyard bomb shelter. *Courtesy of Ypsilanti Archives.*

The program began in mid-November. "Michigan today started plans for dog-tagging its citizens as part of preparations for the possibility of an atom-bomb attack," reported the November 13 *Press*. "What the [state] wants to know is whether people will wear the tags around their necks, carry them in pocketbooks, or toss them aside."

Ypsilanti formed a blood-typing team of local health officials and the city's two Civil Defense coordinators, Harold Haun and Carl Arvin. The group met to choose personnel and the location of blood-typing stations. "The meeting will be the first in which Dan Muntean, recently appointed full time director of the program, has participated," said the November 17 *Press*. "Mr. Muntean, assistant principal of Ypsilanti High School, was granted a 60-day release by the board of education at their meeting Monday night, to take charge of the campaign."

State consultants traveled to Ypsilanti to make recommendations:

> *Conclusions drawn from their visit were that Ypsilanti should have five 5-person teams to successfully type the entire population in a reasonable length of time. Each team is composed of a receptionist, nurse, nurse's aid, and two clerks. Due to the amount of clerical work necessary for each typing, it is deemed necessary to have two clerks to handle the necessary information from each person so as not to slow up the nurse. It was estimated by Chief Haun that...smooth working teams could type a total of 700 to 900 persons a day in Ypsilanti.*

A week later, two five-woman blood-typing teams "attended an orientation meeting Friday afternoon, receiving instructions and suggestions for Monday, the opening day of the program," reported the November 25 *Press*. "Mrs. Jean Smiddy and Mrs. Patricia McGinnis, nurses of the State Office of Civil Defense, spoke to the women, as did Dan Muntean, director of the program in Ypsilanti and Dr. Stacey Howard, chief pathologist of Beyer Hospital and head man for the laboratory phase of the program."

"The two teams will start Monday by taking blood samples from the personnel of Beyer Hospital and will then move on to Cleary College Tuesday where they expect to type well over 200 students," continued the paper. "The blood samples are taken to the laboratory at the rear of Beyer Hospital after each day's run and put into a refrigerator in preparation for typing the following day...[o]f the four duplicate forms which are made out at the time of the taking of the samples, one is given to the person to check against his 'dog tag' when it arrives."

On the twenty-seventh, the paper ran a photo of the first person to be blood-typed: Mayor Dan Quirk, who also led the city's Civil Defense team. The caption noted, "The tiny ribbon on the mayor's shirt front denotes that he has been sampled for typing."

By mid-December, the program was in full swing. "In stops at Beyer Hospital, Cleary College, and Peninsular Paper Mill the week of November 27 to December 1, 1,500 samples were taken; at Michigan State Normal

College and Ypsilanti High School, the total was 2,500; at Estabrook and Prospect Schools and at the Shoppers Stop, 500."

The dog tags were to be distributed early in 1951. "Instead of metal discs," noted the paper, "consideration is being given plastics of varied colors, each corresponding to a type so that work may be speeded in case of disaster. RH factors will be marked on the discs."

One local resident, D., remembers her tags. "I believe I still have mine somewhere," she said in a personal communication, "and I certainly have my parents' tags. At least back then, everyone knew their blood type! As a kid, I thought the tags were kind of neat."

"My husband said they really didn't work," added D. "He was a teenager at the time, and he said the girls exchanged tags with their boyfriends. The girls also liked to decorate them with fingernail polish."

Luckily, Ypsilantians never needed their tags in a disaster. Today, the only vestige of the program are dog tags in dresser drawers, some with creative decoration, from half a century ago.

Top Ten Causes of Death in Local Residents, 1886–1897

Data from five hundred death certificates of Washtenaw County residents reveal that causes of death in the late nineteenth century differ drastically from today. They also suggest a frightening vulnerability to disease without recourse to medicines or, sometimes, competent doctors. When the afflictions are sorted and ranked, the top ten causes of death emerge:

1. Consumption (Tuberculosis)

Consumption was by far the most common cause of death for late nineteenth-century local residents, accounting for a staggering 15 percent of all deaths. Once recognized by Hippocrates as the most prevalent disease in his day, TB had a 40 percent mortality rate. The respiratory disease was so widely feared that when German doctor Robert Koch isolated the bacterium responsible for the disease, he won a 1905 Nobel Prize. In local death records, TB strikes all age groups from late teens to age seventy-five equally, with the striking exception of many children. Tragically, probably almost none of these victims, or their caregivers, knew that the disease was contagious. But they all likely knew at least one Ypsi friend, neighbor or family member who died from the disease. Henry David Thoreau died from TB in 1862 at age forty-four.

2. Scarlet Fever/Scarletina
Although TB did not seem to cause many local children's death, scarlet fever preyed on local children exclusively: all of its victims were between the ages of one and fourteen, with only one older death at age sixty. Named for the red body and facial rash and the "strawberry tongue" it creates, the disease is caused by a strep bacterium and today treated with antibiotics—a scarlet fever vaccine wasn't discovered until the 1920s. Helen Keller, who had perfect sight and hearing at birth, lost both to scarlet fever in 1881 before age two.

3. Heart Disease
One local teen death from heart disease is listed in local records, but most of the victims were in their thirties through their eighties, with the majority in their sixties and seventies. Given the primitive nature of nineteenth-century diagnostic tools, one wonders if the term refers not to disease but to actual heart attacks.

4. Inflammation of the Lungs
This is one of those slippery nineteenth-century medical terms that seems much more like a symptom than an identifiable disease. It would seem to be a symptom of many common nineteenth-century diseases, such as pleurisy, pneumonia or whooping cough. This diagnosis suggests the limits of the age's medical knowledge.

5. Typhoid Fever
This is a nasty one, spread by food or water contaminated by feces and common in the days when people often had sewage "vaults" located directly under their houses or wells and yard privies not too far separate. It can also be spread by asymptomatic carriers. Untreated with modern antibiotics, it has a mortality rate of 10–30 percent. The prevalence of this disease suggests a level of hygiene and sanitation far lower than today.

6. Dropsy
Dropsy is another nineteenth-century term that refers to a symptom, not a disease. It refers to edema, or a swelling of accumulated fluid in some part of the body. It's hard to pinpoint which body part was affected unless the

coroner included such terms as "dropsy of the brain," which might refer to encephalitis. In the county records, there are mentions of plain dropsy, "dropsy of the brain" and "dropsy of the heart," the latter of which might be rheumatic heart disease or congestive heart failure.

7. Cholera Infantum/Summer Complaint
This deadly bacterial disease in hot, moist months struck the tiniest children. All of its local victims were under two years old. The gastrointestinal disease, which could spike fevers up to 104 degrees, was often fatal within twenty-four hours. Pepto-Bismol was originally concocted in the early twentieth century as a medicine—it was originally called Mixture Cholera Infantum. An early ad touts Pepto-Bismol as "An Ideal Mixture for Cholera Infantum and Summer Complaint."

8. Paralysis
The prevalence of this unusual cause of death is striking. Paralysis is a side effect of botulism poisoning. Perhaps these deaths from paralysis were from the effects of undiagnosed botulism poisoning from improperly home-canned food. Likely nearly every home in Ypsi and the township had home-canned food in it—and it's hard to do it right even with modern equipment. Also, the "open kettle" canning technique was common then but is no longer recommended, as it is too dangerous and unsanitary. But it wasn't until the early twentieth century that people began to warn home canners about the danger of open kettle–canned foods. One wonders how widespread undiagnosed botulism was in Ypsilanti.

9. Dysentery
Another digestive system illness, dysentery seems to have struck local victims only from either end of the age spectrum. It also affects victims at either end of their bodies, in a manner better imagined than described. Usually fatal if untreated, it can be spread via contact with public toilets combined with lack of hand-washing.

10. Inflammation of Bowels
This is yet another hazy diagnosis that sounds more like a symptom than a disease. Perhaps it was appendicitis or the gastrointestinal diseases that plagued former residents. It may even be a euphemism.

Local late-nineteenth-century residents bore much in their everyday lives that now are just half-forgotten medical terms. Without antibiotics, many surgical procedures or much understanding of contagion, they were targets for terrible diseases.

But many led long and healthy lives. Aside from these top ten diseases, the second leading cause of death overall was simply old age.

LOVE IN THE YPSILANTI TUBERCULOSIS SANITARIUM

It seems an unlikely setting for romance—a huge halfway house for recovering consumptives. Yet Bertha Wiederhoft's daughter, Rosena, met her intended here, whom she later married.

The "San" offered rest to patients who had been treated for tuberculosis. *Courtesy of Ypsilanti Archives.*

The Ypsilanti After Cure sanitarium, a branch of a big Detroit tuberculosis sanitarium, sat four miles outside the city on Geddes Road. Local historian James Mann recalls seeing it. "I would be driving to Detroit with my father, and there was that big white building we'd always pass."

Inside its walls, consumptives had a chance to rest and help with the hospital's farms, one of eighty and stretching 190 acres. Fresh air and healthy exercise were thought to be beneficial to recovery, and residents planted vegetables, tended chickens and helped make the hospital-farm self-sufficient. Meals included delicious fresh beans, lettuce, tomatoes and other vegetables tended by the patients and often picked the same day.

Built in 1927, the facility was intended not as a hospital to cure tuberculosis but as an after-cure facility, where patients who'd already undergone more aggressive medical intervention could rest and recover

before rejoining the world. The hospital had a capacity of just over 100, and 2,386 patients were treated over its lifetime.

It's likely that, of that number, not everyone recovered but rather succumbed to the disease. And certainly every patient there knew of tuberculosis's deadliness—for years it was the leading killer in Washtenaw County. Yet against this grim backdrop, Rosena and a male patient, Thomas Green, found each other and later built a life together.

The facility closed on May 7, 1954, as improved public health reduced the specter of TB. The remaining patients were sent to other institutions, and the farmland was put up for sale. After twenty-seven years, the "San" was, thankfully, no longer needed. Rosena went on to have a daughter, Diane, and died in 1998 after a life spanning almost all of the twentieth century.

In its clean, fresh environment, the San had not only restored Rosena's life but also given her the opportunity to join it with another.

MALARIA IN WASHTENAW COUNTY

Don't go to Michigan, land of ills
The name means ague, fever, and chills.
—popular nineteenth-century saying

In September 1824, twenty-year-old Irish immigrant Walter Oakman bought 123 acres of land near Ypsilanti. Thirteen days later, he died of malaria (according to a timeline of early Ypsilanti history by Paulette Quartermain), the first recorded death in Washtenaw County.

In 1829—according to the Biographical Publishing Company's Portrait and Biographical Album of Washtenaw County, Michigan—on a farm northwest of Ann Arbor, schoolboy Daniel Hiscock "assisted his father in clearing the farm, grubbing stumps for other people, and drove a team comprising four yoke of cattle, at the same time shaking like a leaf with the ague."

In 1831, Pennsylvania emigrant John Ansley collapsed on the side of the road to Ann Arbor. "We had not accomplished more than half our journey," his wife, Philena Ansley, later wrote, "when my husband was taken with the fever and ague, and was obliged to lie down by the roadside and wait the approach of some person with a team, or until he should be able to proceed on foot."

The disease the settlers called "the ague" (pronounced "ag-yew," from the Latin *febris acuta*, "sharp fever") is one of the oldest-known human plagues, described by Herodotus. It is now known as malaria, and it is still the leading cause of death on the planet. Though now largely confined to the tropics, in the infant United States malaria was common as far north as New England. Endemic in the then-swampy Michigan, it was a leading cause of sickness in nineteenth-century Washtenaw County.

The 1836 Calhoun County settler Anson Van Buren described the disease as a chill that "crept over your system in streaks, faster and faster, and then colder and colder in succeeding undulations that coursed down your back." The chills caused shaking so violent that "the dishes rattled on the shelves against the log wall." Afterward came fever, sweat and relief. Then the cycle repeated, sometimes for months.

Farmers scheduled their lives around the sickness, saving strenuous tasks like plowing for "well" days. Even professionals found it hard to work on their "ague" days, as a minister learned when he was stuck by the fever when he was scheduled to preside at a wedding. "In the morning he attempted to fortify himself by taking a large dose of quinine and at noon repeated the precaution by taking a larger dose, and by the time the wedding party arrived, the justice was delirious," according to the 1880 edition of the Michigan Historical Collections, by the Michigan State Historical Society, the Pioneer Society of the State of Michigan and the Michigan Historical Commission. The official was "taken to the well and drenched with cold water, and for a short time, consciousness returned, and seizing that moment the parties were married."

Made from the bark of the Peruvian cinchona tree, quinine subdued malaria's worst symptoms. But for most of the nineteenth century it remained scarce and expensive, so people tried all kinds of alternatives. One Michigan doctor wrote that he found "a tea or decoction made from the poplar and iron wood bark to answer a very good purpose" and also made a "cure" with tarry extract of butternut bark, though he admitted that patients who tried it often told him "that they much preferred the disease to the remedy."

Ann Arbor druggist Dr. A.W. Chase's famous 1863 compendium, *Information for Everybody*, offers no fewer than a dozen do-it-yourself ague cures, one brewed from mandrake root and another supplied by a clairvoyant. Many commercial cures concocted by nostrum-mongers contained quinine in more or less random amounts, adulterated with substances ranging from wintergreen to molasses. "Rhodes' Fever and Ague Cure" vowed to protect "any resident or traveler…from any ague or Bilious disease whatever, or any injury from constantly inhaling Malaria or Miasma." Chemist O.L. Churchill reported that Rhodes' "cure" contained no quinine, but only charcoal, glucose, alcohol, iron and muriatic acid—a corrosive today used to "pickle" steel and make mustard gas. Even worse was the "Anti-Chill Pill," whose recipe contained arsenic. No wonder some sufferers opted instead for a curative slug of whiskey, one man regarding it as "necessary as a means of keeping off the pond ague."

From 1868 to 1882, forty-eight county residents died of malaria. Because the cold-tolerant strain of the disease that was likely prevalent here has a fatality rate of about 1 percent, the deaths imply thousands of sufferers. In 1887, the Ann Arbor Business Men's Association published a guide to the Ann Arbor that declared, "The whole place is entirely free of malaria." But in fact, more than sixty years after Walter Oakman's death, the disease was apparently far from conquered. Nearly every edition of the weekly *Ann Arbor Courier* that year carried an ad for Tutt's Pills: "In malarial districts their virtues are widely recognized, as they possess peculiar properties in freeing the system from that poison." A competing product, "Ayer's Ague Cure," was advertised in the August 3, 1887 edition. Even ten years later, the June 4, 1897 edition of the *Ann Arbor Argus* contains a large ad, headlined "Shakes," for Scott's Emulsion of Cod-Liver Oil with hypophosphites to combat "a genuine malarial chill."

By then, though, the worst was over. By 1890, large-scale cinchona cultivation was underway in Indonesia, drastically reducing the price of quinine. And in 1897, British officer Ronald Ross discovered the malarial role of the anopheles mosquito, for which he won the 1902 Nobel Prize. Malaria, it turned out, was caused by the microparasite plasmodium cycling between humans and mosquitoes. Though a vaccine remains elusive to this day, Ross's discovery showed how malaria could be controlled by draining mosquito breeding sites and applying pesticides. By the early twentieth century, the infectious cycle was broken in the once-swampy Michigan.

Then, in 1925, the U-M brought it back. Austrian psychiatrist Julius Wagner-Jauregg had found that high malarial fevers seemed to alleviate the symptoms of advanced syphilis. The discovery earned him the Nobel for 1927, the second of four Nobels eventually awarded for malaria work.

Following the New York State Psychiatric Institute and the Mayo Clinic, the U-M began a program of "malarial fever therapy," in which patients were injected with malaria-contaminated blood. It remained the state-of-the-art therapy for advanced syphilis until penicillin supplanted it after World War II.

In 1947, the newly organized Centers for Disease Control launched a nationwide campaign to eradicate malaria. By applying the pesticide DDT to millions of rural homes, malaria was eliminated as a significant public health problem within two years.

Similar eradication efforts in tropical countries failed, however, and were eventually abandoned. The CDC estimates that malaria still kills 1 million people a year, most of them young children in sub-Saharan Africa. Only in the past few years has the infection again become a global public health focus. This April, United Nations secretary general Ban Ki-moon called for making malaria control measures, such as insecticide-treated bed nets, available throughout Africa by the end of 2010. It's an ambitious goal, but if it succeeds, malaria may finally became just a historical footnote there as well.

Part III

Good Times

The Concrete Origins of Ypsilanti's Heritage Festival

It all started with a sidewalk.

The completion of the nice, new sidewalks and street repaving in 1978 Depot Town didn't seem like much of an event to some. Not compared to the Rolling Stones' July concert at Detroit's Masonic Hall or the release of the hot new summer movie *Grease*, playing at Briarwood, or even the upcoming Drum Corps championship at Rynearson Stadium.

And it wasn't—until the Depot Town Association, led by President Tom Dodd, hit on the idea of transforming a mundane municipal improvement into a whimsical "Sidewalk Celebration."

DTA member and artist Carolyn McKeever drew an elegant old-timey poster, and the festival was on!

Visitors could look forward to such delights as "Plain and Fancy Walking," bluegrass and jazz and the excitement of ceremonial sidewalk dedications and ribbon-cutting, by no less an eminence than "Hizzoner" Mayor Goodman. There was even a beer garden and a "Color T.V. Raffle." Activities were planned from noon until dark.

"Dancing to live band music, exhibits from art to history, old-time movies, buggy rides, and more will enliven Depot Town tomorrow," reported the July 14 *Ypsilanti Press*. "City officials, including Mayor George Goodman and

"Plain and Fancy Walkin'" was a highlight of the tiny festival. *Courtesy of Ypsilanti Archives.*

City Manager Steve Shutt, will dedicate concrete and asphalt wherever they encounter ribbons to be cut on a route from the Alibi Bar [now Aubree's] lot to the Huron River, then back to the railroad."

"'It's going to be a wide-open party; we're telling the community to come down and play with us,' said Dodd." Aside from the beer garden, most of the activities were free.

The day after the festival, the *Press* ran a picture of a crowd in Depot Town. "There was music, there was dancing, there were draft horses prancing," read a caption, "and it all took place Saturday in Depot Town during the Sidewalk Celebration. When sunny skies and lots of heat helped bring out the crowds, they found plenty to do and see." On Monday, the *Press* ran more pictures—of the musicians Stoney Creek, dancers from Ann Arbor's A-Squares, a classic car and a food tent.

"During all that local hoopla," said Dodd in a personal e-mail, "Rich Baird [of the Visitors and Convention Bureau], Nathalie Edmunds, and I stopped in to the Eagles Hall for a moment of air conditioning and posited on how we ought to have this kind of a celebration as an annual event."

The next year, in 1979, Ypsilanti organizations along with a horde of volunteers planned to repeat and expand the event, renaming it the Ypsilanti Yesteryear Heritage Fest. An August 19, 1979 *Press* editorial urged residents to attend. "On the basis of the enthusiastic support of thousands who will participate in what is hoped to be an annual event, the Friday, Saturday, and Sunday event should be a blockbuster of fun."

The *Press* boosted Heritage Days by including an iron-on T-shirt decal so that readers could make their own shirts. It also printed an elaborate souvenir program packed with information about the events and such well-written historical essays as a story about four nineteenth-century firms still in existence in 1979: Peninsular Paper, the National Bank of Ypsilanti, Mellencamp's and the city's oldest business, Mack & Mack Furniture.

The slate of events featured some with a charming home-grown quality, such as the frog-jumping contest, kids' field events and a contest to make one's own float and race down the river. The range of fun, free events, combined with mild, seventy-degree weather, resulted in an unprecedented turnout of fifty thousand attendees, raising about $200,000.

Now in its thirty-first year, Heritage Fest attracts about 100,000 visitors and offers an even greater, if not dizzying, range of delightful things to do, including the popular "Nightmare Cruise," historical walks with Ypsi city historian James Mann and a chance to see Buffalo Soldier reenactors and even taste kettle-brewed beer.

"Today, folks down in Depot Town often refer to the celebrants as 'Yesterfesters,'" said Dodd. When you wander over to Depot Town, take a quick peek at the sidewalks—where it all began.

VOTE NO! ON ANTI-BUTTER PROPOSAL 4!

I strive to remain above the political fray.

But one proposal on the November ballot mandates that I speak out in the interest of all that is good and right.

Proposal 4 asks that the sale of yellow-colored oleomargarine be permitted in this state, whose economic bedrock is the dairy industry.

Take a look at this pro-butter advertisement. Admire the, er, sophisticated graphic design. Note that "Butter" is the keystone of the Michigan agricultural arch, which consists of such goodies as ice cream, condensed milk and "fluid milk," with "soil conservation" thrown in for good measure.

Given these facts, can you, kind reader, feed your Michigan children oleomargarine in good conscience? At present, you can buy oleomargarine in the familiar plastic bag with a capsule of colorant. You know the drill: you have to squoosh the bag so that the included capsule breaks and the colorant spreads throughout the disgusting oleo, rendering it yellow.

What a waste of time and energy when patriotic Michigan families can buy good, pure butter without the need to adulterate it with fancy dyes.

Another ad proclaims "Protect Yourself and Family!"—rendered in a sturdy, sensible font. Beneath the order "Protect Your Own," the ad reads, "The first year Canada allowed substitutes to be colored yellow in imitation of butter cost Dairy Farmers there 50 million dollars. That can happen in Michigan…where 600,000 people depend on Dairying for their livelihood…with an investment TWICE THAT OF THE ENTIRE WORLD OPERATIONS OF THE FORD MOTOR COMPANY!"

Surely you, kind reader, would not want to be responsible for bankrupting thousands of dairymen in our noble state.

Proposal 4 means that pre-colored oleo will be available in stores, without the tedious bag-squooshing. How will you know this artificial, factory-concocted substance is pure? Who knows what will be in there? Likely a vile mishmash of impure and cheap substances—is that good enough for your child's toast? I truly doubt it.

In all fairness, I here include three pro-oleo ads in addition to the pro-butter material. Note that the first pro-oleo ad presumes a general level of literacy in a butter-fed populace sufficient to recognize the reference to "Simon Legree." This literacy level will be lost if we switch from edifying butter to enervating margarine. Would you be content to see your children

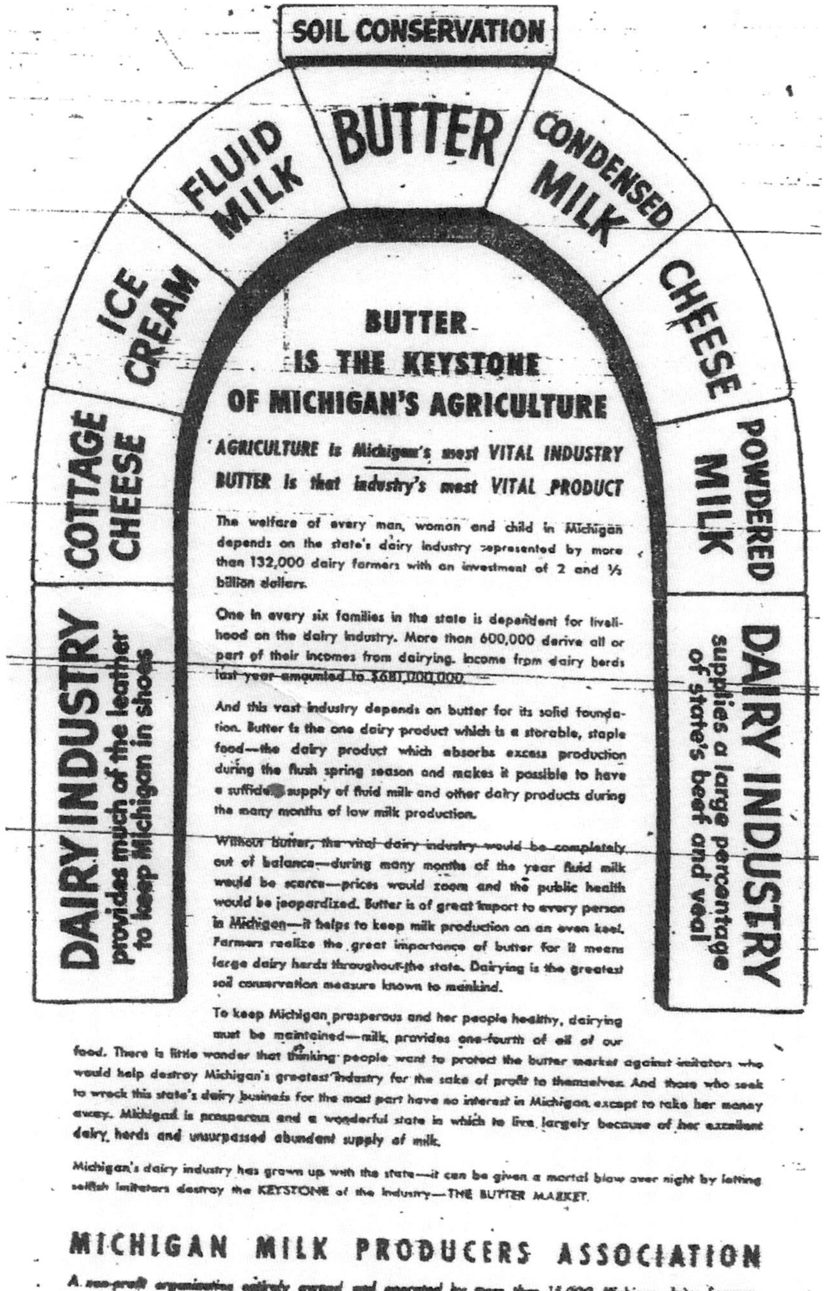

This ad's copywriter wrote, "This vast industry depends on butter for its solid foundation." *Courtesy of Ypsilanti Archives.*

The margariners invoked *Uncle Tom's Cabin* in support of yellow oleo. *Courtesy of Ypsilanti Archives.*

Billie Burke Compares Blue Bonnet —Always Puts It On!

Here's a hint from Billie Burke. Compare BLUE BONNET Margarine with *any* spread at *any* price. Like the famous movie star, you'll love BLUE BONNET's fresh, sweet *flavor!* Rich *nutrition!* Real *economy!* BLUE BONNET is America's fine-quality *all vegetable* margarine. But it costs only about half as much as the high-priced spread for bread! BLUE BONNET colors in 2 minutes flat—it comes in the famous Yellow Quik bag. So buy BLUE BONNET and get "all three"—Flavor! Nutrition! Econom-e-e!

Blue Bonnet ran a series of ads featuring celebrities wearing the Blue Bonnet. *Courtesy of Ypsilanti Archives.*

sink from butter-fed, Shakespeare-quoting prodigies to margarine-mumbling idiots? I didn't think so. Vote No on Proposal 4.

You can see that the margariners don't hesitate to sink to celebrity endorsements.

Note the moving picture star Billie Burke wearing the traitorous Blue Bonnet. Do you, neighbor, decide what's good for your family based on what some moving picture star says? Did our pioneer forefathers make decisions based on the opinions of flibbertigibbet entertainers? No sir; they were too busy building up our state into a dairy stronghold.

Would you sully your table with a dubious substance that Billie Burke here advocates—advocates for a payment given her by the margariners?

The margariners ridicule our revered ancestors. *Courtesy of Ypsilanti Archives.*

No sir; you have more sense and gristle that that. You don't let some pretty "movie star" dictate what wholesome foods you feed to your children. Do you? Vote NO on Proposal 4.

Note that the pro-oleo folks disparage Grandpa in their last ad. The man who hewed down trees for your ancestral log cabin among the howling Michigan wolves. The man who churned butter from the milk cow to tide his family through a desperate Michigan winter. The man who made sumac ice cream for the delight of his little ones—little ones who in turn gave birth to and raised you, kind reader.

Can you, in good conscience, vote against these pioneer values? Can you spit on your grandfather's grave? I thought not. This November 1950, vote NO on Proposal 4.

A Brief History of Scholastic Inebriation

The periodic flap over University of Michigan student drinking is nothing new. This activity extends far back into the history of early Ypsilanti papers. One 1910 account details the riotous visit of rowdy Ann Arbor students to the demure, tea-drinking town of Ypsilanti. It was quite a shock to our quiet city.

However, alert police work by our capable officers gently dissuaded the miscreants from wreaking further damage. With typical Ypsilanti generosity, we even gave one gentleman free overnight accommodations in one of our most popular lodging houses!

"A University fraternity, reported to be the Chi Psi, came here Friday evening to initiate one of their members," reported the December 10, 1910 *Ypsilanti Daily Press*. "The fraternity had rented the basement of the Hawkins House where the initiation took place. A little keg party was one of the closing features of the initiation."

Cheered by their brotherly quaffing, the fraternity members left the hotel determined to raise a hearty salute to their host city.

First, they tried to enter a dance in the Ypsilanti Armory. When told it was by invitation only, they waited until the dance ended and then had words with the manager, William Daley. Daley politely remonstrated with the men but was forced to call for aid from local police and swear out a warrant for their arrest. The group fled.

Next, the men decided it would be the height of rebellion to steal a car! They snagged one outside a downtown restaurant, Bonnie and Clyde–style (except for the Bonnie), and drove it to the railroad depot, a delirious rampage of half a mile. There they parked it. Mission accomplished!

The evening's denouement came when the group entered a downtown laundry. The frightened proprietor fled as the students indulged in depraved debauchery by doing some laundry. Unfortunately, their inexperience with the subtler arts of Ypsilanti laundry techniques resulted in their breaking a couple of things.

One of the students, George Cramer, was arrested. "He pleaded guilty [to assault and battery] and was fined the costs, $5.15," said the *Press*. "He also paid Hing Wing $4 for breaking some of the machinery in his laundry on Washington Street."

Two days later, the fraternity denied everything. "They point to the absurdity of a fraternity leaving a well furnished house to hold an initiation in another city," reported the December 12 *Ypsilanti Daily Press*.

"Just who the offenders were, no one thus far seems able to determine," noted the paper. "This much is positive, however—the visitors were here, considerable disgraceful disturbance was created, the Chinaman was badly scared, the laundry machine was broken and one young fellow was released [after paying for] the crippled shirt polisher."

At least the students got home safely. Another student in 1932 wasn't as lucky. "[U-M student] John Kulick…is drinking hot lemonade and swallowing quinine tablets today as result of a reluctant outing in Prospect Park at 1:30 this morning," said the April 11, 1932 *Ypsilanti Daily Press*. "He told police that he had been forcibly removed from his bed, his head wrapped in a blanket, and had been left in the park here after being driven around in an automobile."

The paper continued, "His pajama clad figure attracted the attention of Sergeant Ernest Klavitter and Patrolman Laidlaw who saw to it that he obtained a ride to Ann Arbor with four men who were going that way."

Once again, Ypsilantians extended courtesy to visiting wayward youth. "Kulick had borrowed a pair of slippers and a robe at 611 North Prospect St. before police found him."

One U-M student encountered a less charitable response in Ann Arbor. Since the May 22, 1937 *Ypsilanti Daily Press* article "Impetuous Youth Puts Flavor into Government Work" cannot be improved upon, it is hereby quoted in its entirety:

> *Every now and then novel ideas concerning the proper method of carrying out government services are born in a student's mind, and with the impetuosity*

that gives youth its charm and gets it in occasional trouble, an attempt is usually made to put them into practice.

This may have been true in the case of one Robert David, who at the age of 20 has formed some ideas of how to make the dull and routine envelopes in which students receive their daily mail more interesting and novel in appearance.

In pursuance of this idea, and apparently wishing to get an early start on his work, he began at one o'clock this morning to pour catsup in the mailbox at E. Liberty and S. Fourth Sts. and was really warming to his work when he noticed a police officer who had come up behind him and who was watching the process not without interest, although definitely lacking in appreciative approval.

As a result of the officer's reaction Mr. Davis was considering the merits of his plan in the county jail this morning where he is awaiting arraignment in justice court on charges of intoxication and disorderly conduct.

For all the depredations these U-M students committed, even this Ypsilantian has a grudging respect for their creativity. Show me one modern-day U-M student who expresses his tipsiness by kidnapping one of his brethren and abandoning him in his pajamas in a distant park or crippling a shirt polisher or seasoning mail.

And modern students merely want to get drunk? Amateurs!

Luminous Pork Chop Comes to Light

Unlike today's Ypsilantians worried about swine flu, local citizens of the past had a different pig-related concern.

They read this story, emanating from nearby Jackson, in the Tuesday, September 26, 1950 *Ypsilanti Daily Press*. It is transcribed here as a cautionary tale:

Science, as well as the neighbors, is keenly interested in Russell Mitchell's glowing pork chop.

Mitchell stumbled on the phenomenon of the refrigerator last week. It actually is a pork chop that glows in the dark.

The Jackson Citizen-Patriot *explained that the luminous chop "came to light" in an unusual circumstance when Russell opened the refrigerator at his home in a darkened kitchen. The bulb inside the box was burned out. There in the dark, however, was the pork chop, casting its rich and brilliant glow.*

Russell couldn't believe it. He phoned his mother, Mrs. Ida Mitchell, who operates the Jackson County Building telephone switchboard. Together they examined the pork chop. When they removed it from the wax paper wrapping they had luminous marks on their hands. Then they were convinced their eyes weren't deceiving them.

Fearing that the meat might be contaminated and worried lest there might be ill effects from three others they had eaten that were bought at the same time, Mrs. Mitchell called in the city health department. Sanitarian Dale Brooks hadn't ever seen anything like it. But he was intensely interested in a laboratory explanation of the phenomenon.

Federal meat inspectors in Detroit had never heard of anything like it. Neither had the chief veterinarian of the Chicago Board of health.

The Citizen-Patriot *asked Dr. J.H. Ahronheim, Foote Hospital pathologist, to examine the meat.*

Dr. Ahronheim said today a microscopic examination convinced him that the glow emanated from tiny organisms which produced a phosphorescence due to decay.

The pork chop, Dr. Ahronheim said, was heavy with bacteria of a type not harmful if consumed.

Mrs. Mitchell and Russell breathed a sigh of relief.

It is interesting to note the legion of experts summoned to shed light on this tiny cutlet, while it shed light on them: Jackson city health department sanitarian Dale Brooks; federal meat inspectors in Detroit; the Chicago Board of Health chief veterinarian; and Jackson's Foote Hospital pathologist J.H. Ahronheim.

In short, medical men from three cities, in two states, were consulted on this question. Note also that the eminent Dr. J.H. Ahronheim apparently took several full days to subject the meat bit to extensive tests—the original discovery of the chop, this Tuesday-published story says, was "last week." The newspaper editors must have waited with bated breath for the resolution of the story and indeed published it the same day the doctor released his findings.

Note that the doctor has informed thousands of newspaper readers that a luminous pork chop is no cause for concern. Fire up the frying pan!

You Use Witch Sugar?

The beet men economizing on the ad budget. *Courtesy of Ypsilanti Archives.*

Sometimes you see an ad whose picture and text go together so well that you think, "Wow—what a great match!" This is not one of those times.

"Let's see, what image should we, the Farmers and Manufacturers Beet Sugar Association, associate with our underdog product, Michigan Made Beet Sugar? Smiling children spooning sugar into their tea? A happy mom adding sugar to cookie dough? A gruff yet lovable dad putting sugar on his oatmeal? No, we have a better idea for branding beet sugar into the public consciousness."

This ad has the same "in-house" quality as did the dairy farmers' pro-butter ad from the Oleo Wars in the 1950s. I doubt either agricultural organization had the cash to hire a snazzy New York ad firm. The fonts are sturdy, the images are earnest and the conception is a tad low on the wow factor.

Nevertheless, readers, aside from these quibbles, please join me in supporting Depression-era beet farmers. Next time you're in Meijer's or Krogers, go to the customer service area. Slap your hand firmly on the counter and bellow, "Give me Michigan Made Beet Sugar and no other kind!" Then storm out. Join me in boosting Michigan Made Beet Sugar!

Boosting Michigan Made Beet Sugar is best done by thrusting your fist into the air randomly throughout your day—on the bus, in the office, at the family dinner table—and yelling, "BEET SUGAR! BEET SUGAR! BEET SUGAR!" This cooperation will not cost you an extra penny. Michigan Made Beet Sugar: available in the convenient one-hundred-pound sack!

YPSILANTI'S GOLDEN AGE OF FREE PARKING: 1900–1942

From around the turn of the century, when a few cars began appearing on Ypsilanti streets (most of them unpaved), to World War II, when the streets faced an influx of Bomber Plant workers' cars, parking in the city was free.

It just hadn't occurred to anyone to charge for it.

During World War II, the Ypsilanti Salvage Committee held huge scrap metal and rubber drives. Housewives were even told to save pan drippings from roasted meats, for "scrap fat" used to make glycerin for the war effort. The entire city was economizing and doing without. Perhaps it was this atmosphere of frugal austerity that led the city to seek more sources of revenue.

"Ypsilanti's 300 parking meters are today being installed and will go into effect at 9 a.m. Thursday," announced the July 8, 1942 *Ypsilanti Daily Press*.

"Instructions for their use are found on the meters themselves. Cars may park for 12 minutes for one cent, 24 minutes for two cents, 36 minutes for 3 cents and 60 minutes for a nickel." The metered time was 9:00 a.m. to 6:00 p.m. every weekday and 9:00 a.m. to 9:00 p.m. on Saturdays.

The paper went into detail about the workings of the mysterious meters:

> *The meters are automatic; only the insertion of a coin or coins being necessary to start meter operating. Deposit of the coin brings into view a clock face with hand ticking off the minutes. At the end of the allotted time the clock face and indicator drop from sight and patrolling officers can see that the car is illegally parked...Meters in Ypsilanti have been installed for a six months trial period. If found unsatisfactory at that time, they will be removed.*

In addition to the instructions printed on the meter and the newspaper's explanation, "booklets explaining the use of meters are now being distributed at various business places about the city where motorists may secure them."

The next day, as the *Press* reported:

> *Strange and interesting were the reactions of motorists this morning as they surveyed the city's new parking meters.*
>
> *Some walked slowly toward the meters, viewing them skeptically. Others tried not to look as foolish and inexperienced as they felt while*

> *reading instructions on the meter. The "old hands" walked with a confident stride, and in businesslike fashion inserted their coins and were on their way. And many were still either coldly surveying the machines and refusing "to play" or else dashed off without so much as a look in the direction of the meters.*

Adoption of the meters was not immediate. "A check within the first hour that meters were in effect showed 21 violations out of 50 cars. Violations were by no means confined to side streets either, for a considerable number were counted on Michigan Ave. Even the nearness to the police station didn't frighten some, for there was little legal-sounding ticking in meters in the same block as police headquarters."

The city was abuzz with debate about the new machine, which "furnished a new topic for conversation…motorists were seen and heard discussing the relative merits of the new devices."

A week and a half later, Chief of Police Dan Patch informed city council that the meters were expected to bring in between $1,200 and $1,500 in July. Officer Perry Burrell was given the meter coin-collection beat and soon gained meter savvy. The July 21 *Press* noted, "[Burrell says] use old nickels in preference to new five cent pieces, as the old ones work better in the meters."

Police Chief Dan Patch's prediction was correct. By August, the meters had collected $1,648.78 in revenue. After deducting the cost of installation and Officer Burrell's $180 per month salary, the meters netted the city $412.60 ($5,400 in today's dollars).

Faced with this profit, city officials' talk about removing the meters after six months vanished, and Ypsilantians have been digging into their pockets for coins ever since.

Chrysler Record Players and the Potato Car

With automakers regularly rolling out new models with amazing features, here's a peek at offbeat automotive snippets of the past.

In 1956–57, Chrysler experimented with installing record players in cars. In the first year, 3,685 buyers opted for this novelty; in the second (and final) year of the program, only 675 did.

"The needle on that system came down from above onto the record and one of the chief complaints was that the needle jumped when the car went over bumps," reported the May 3, 1965 *Ypsilanti Press.*

"In 1960–61, Chrysler used a different type record player which was installed in the glove compartment. In this unit, the needle was pointed upward and the record was lowered to it, thus reducing the amount of distortion. The system never really caught on and was dropped."

The article also details the exciting new development of cigar box–sized eight-track players to appear in 1966 Ford cars. Motorola made the players, RCA provided the music and the Lear Jet Corporation "set up a Detroit plant to build tape cartridges and make tapes."

Chrysler's automotive record player probably worked best while driving at slow speeds, but sometimes slowness was a problem. In the summer of 1921, the Ann Arbor Automobile Club petitioned city council to increase downtown speeds from ten to fifteen miles per hour and from fifteen to twenty miles on the city's outskirts. Quoted in the *Ypsilanti Daily Press*, the club said that "the slow speed has two evil results: it tends to congestion and to law breaking." The group pointed out that the higher proposed speeds conformed to Michigan state law that mandated fifteen miles per hour in cities' business sections and twenty in residential areas.

"City Attorney Bonisteel, who was present," added the paper, "told the auto people that they would find the common council fair-minded on the proposition. 'Present your arguments for conformity to the state law, regulating traffic in cities, and I think the probabilities are that they will adopt your view.'"

With cars speeding up, it was necessary to ensure safety, but Ypsilanti's efforts to regulate traffic were improvisatory, as the December 20, 1930 *Ypsilanti Daily Press* noted:

> *When the patient public of Ypsilanti becomes aroused, there is reason to believe that the complaint is justified.*
>
> *For some time the matter of traffic regulation in Ypsilanti has been an experiment manipulated according to the fancies of whatever group of men happened to have charge of that particular branch of city affairs.*
>
> *Mushroom lights came first and after several had been installed at considerable expense, their uselessness was finally recognized and they were discontinued as signals, although several remain for motorists to dodge and for pedestrians to stumble over.*

> *Next came a shipment of stop signs to be scattered around the city. Some served as a traffic aid, others as a hindrance. They are still in effect and so long as the police department exercises judgment in enforcement of the Stop Street ordinance, there is little objection. To compel every motorist to stop at every Stop sign regardless of the time of day or the traffic condition at any particular point would be ridiculous.*

The article went on to complain about "the preposterous and most exasperating traffic signal in Ypsilanti," a light on Michigan Avenue at Park Street, erected to protect schoolchildren but unnecessarily slowing down Michigan Avenue traffic outside of school-crossing hours.

Also in 1930, local car companies were doing their best to motivate sales during the Depression. Some of the most strident advertisements in town came from the E.G. Wiedman Auto Company, at 212 Pearl Street (where the downtown bus stop is today).

"Wiedman is offering the greatest values in years," noted an ad. "Plenty of cars to choose from—each and every one priced at a real low price." The special, a 1930 Ford Coupe, was offered for $195 ($2,500 today).

But an even better deal came about three years later, when Otto Hopp obtained a car for mere peanuts—or, rather, potatoes.

"A car belonging to Elmer and Elaine Avery, Railroad St., is claimed to have been loaned to Otto Hopp, Saline Rd., for 30 days," read the March 17, 1933 *Ypsilanti Daily Press*. "In return Avery was to receive several bushels of vegetables and potatoes."

"Mr. Hopp claimed that he understood that he had purchased the car, but had never received the title. In settling the dispute it was decided that the title to the machine would be surrendered to Mr. Hopp and Mr. Avery would receive 10 bushels of potatoes and $1 in cash."

Now, those were some valuable taters!

Five Must-Have Appliances

A sneak peek at some of the latest lovely, practical and labor-saving devices for your home. Be the first on your block to snag one of these beauties!

1. Gasoline Stove
How wasteful it is to cook on an electric stove! There's no precision, your best dishes get burnt and it's nothing but frustration. At least, it was, till your sweetie surprised you with your new 1888 Gasoline Stove!

It's easy to use. Merely fill the uplifted can with fresh gasoline—whoops, turn the burner off, there—that's better—and put the lid on tight. Tighter than that. Wipe that little drip off, there. And there you go—you're off on a new culinary adventure! Don't forget to have a quick chat with your

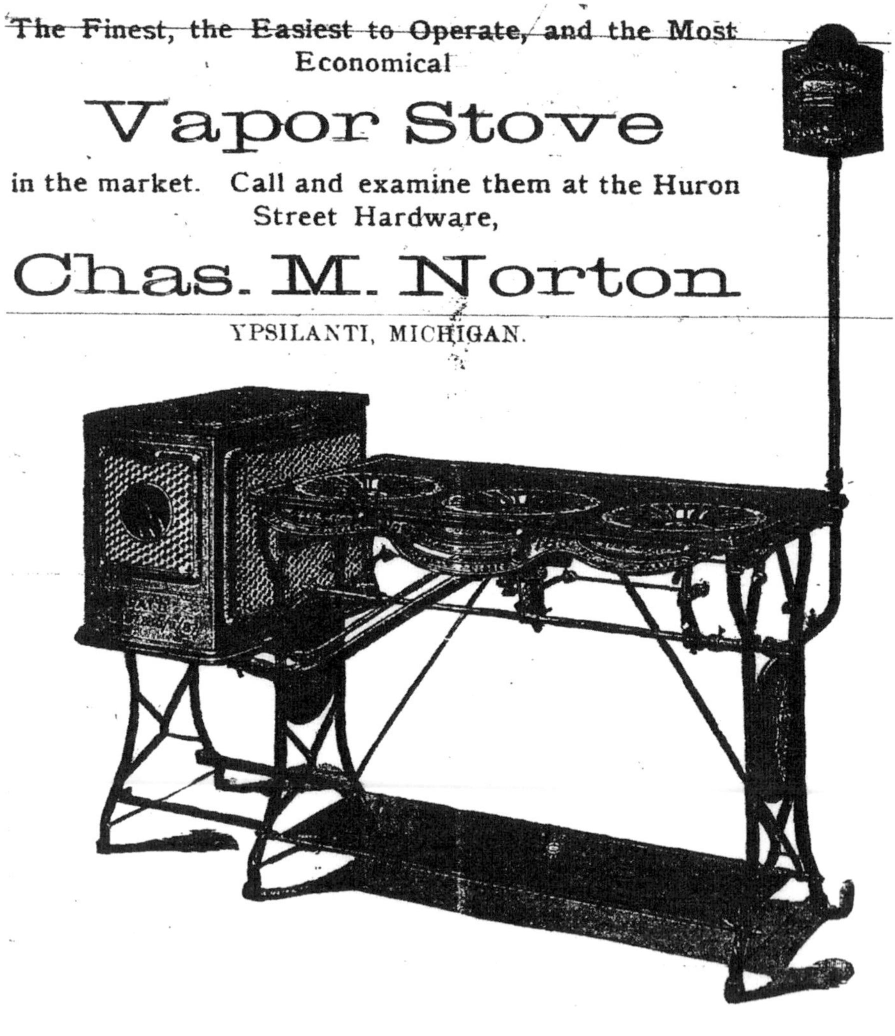

Vapor stoves could burn several fuels, including gasoline, and made cooking exciting.

insurance agent. Just wait till the ladies at church lay eyes on the gourmet creations you'll effortlessly whip up on your Gasoline Stove!

Better get yours today while supplies last. They're stylish and snazzy! They're not just hot—they're incendiary!

2. Sanitary House Closet

Sewer connection a bit iffy? Have you considered an elegant 1903 House Closet?

It has delicate embroidery on the plush upholstered lid and the graceful woodwork. The House Closet bespeaks good taste—it's certainly far more refined than those citified porcelain bowls.

It's discreet and noiseless and perfectly sanitary, too—with the "odorless receptacle cover, no germs can possibly affect the air." So attractive you'll use it as a chair even when you're not—erm—not using it as a chair.

3. Pneumatic Cleaner

You know how it is with kids. The lovely nutritious meal you slaved over ends up in crumbs all over the floor. Don't fret. Whip out your handy forty-pound barrel-shaped 1910 Regina Pneumatic Cleaner. It does all of the work for you! Just pump vigorously on the long handle while pushing the durable, solid metal vacuum head over your rug with the other hand. To give your children healthful exercise, ask them to pump and make it a game—tell them to pretend they're galley slaves pulling an oar. The powerful double bellows inside the Cleaner's barrel whisks away those crumbs in a trice. When you're done, stash this compact model in any small space.

4. Indoor Gasoline Torch

Power out again? Not a problem for someone as well prepared as you.

Just light the 1903 Gasoline Torch mounted directly over your reading chair and settle back for a pleasant evening under its "large, brilliant white flame."

It's convenient—the reservoir holds a generous six quarts of gasoline, so you only have to fill it once in a while.

And it's well designed—the burner is only a short distance from the reservoir, so there's no straining to reach any part.

As a bonus, it pleases the senses, as you enjoy the delightful fragrance of burning gasoline filling your home.

5. Home Incinerator
Oh, how the trash piles up! Ever since the war ended and they started making all those plastic things, it's such a bother to get rid of them all. Or it is for some people, maybe—not you!

Plastic shampoo bottles, cling wrap, the broken toy—no need to wait for the rubbish man, like less foresighted folks, when you can toss it all in your own home incinerator! See how quickly the clean, pure gas flashes on, reducing your trash to ashes in seconds and producing a strong, distinctive scent—the scent of modernity! You can use the ashes on your garden, too.

Don't you see how happy a housewife could be? You, too, can be that happy, someday—with a Gas Incinerator. Call your friendly Michigan Consolidated Gas Company man today.

Beyer Memorial Hospital's 1950s Newspaper

You might not think a half-century-old hospital newsletter would be the most exciting accidental find while researching a story on polio.

But in the 1950s, Beyer Hospital produced a newspaper whose quality, depth and scope would be worthy of a town the size of Belleville. With articles typed on typewriters and assembled in the time-honored cut, paste and photocopy style, the *Beyer Banner* unexpectedly enchants the reader with five salient qualities:

1. The paper contains stories you'd never read anywhere else. One explains that the different styles of caps among nurses at Beyer are due to each nursing school having its own distinctive cap, not unlike the traditional regimental or club necktie.

"Represented at Bayer are 56 schools by 56 different caps," notes an article. "The nurses wearing these caps come from hospitals and university nursing schools located in practically all of the 48 United States." U-M's official nursing cap, pictured in the top left photo opposite, is a plain, pointy model.

2. The little in-house paper took itself seriously. It had an official masthead listing an editor, assistant editor, an editorial committee of three and no fewer than a dozen reporters, most of them heads of the various hospital

NURSES CAPS
SEEN AT BEYER MEMORIAL HOSPITAL

Patients and employees in hospitals have long been confused by the girls in white; which one is an aid, a practical nurse, or a registered nurse?

The registered nurse always wears a cap. She may be distinguished from the practical nurse by her cap because the practical always has a wide gray band on a starched white cap.

The registered nurse's cap will vary in size, material and shape, starched or organdy, and the band will also vary in color and size or be without a band entirely.

The nurses' cap is the symbol of their profession and establishes a tradition for each school.

Represented at Beyer are 56 schools by 56 different caps. The nurses wearing these caps come from hospitals and university nursing schools located in practically all of the 48 United States.

University of Michigan, Ann Arbor, Michigan; Bishop Clarkson Memorial Hospital, Omaha, Nebraska; Grace Hospital, Detroit, Michigan; St. Anthony's, Rockford, Illinois; Henry Ford Hospital, Detroit, Michigan; Abbott Hospital, Minneapolis, Minn.; St. John's Hospital, Fargo, North Dakota; Indianapolis General, Indianapolis, Indiana; Read Memorial Hospital, Richmond, Indiana; Foote Memorial Hospital, Jackson, Michigan; Reading Hospital, Reading, Pa.; Sewickley Valley Hospital, Sewickley Pa.

Evanston Hospital, Evanston, Illinois; St. Luke's Hospital, New York, New York; Sibley Memorial Hospital, Washington, D.C.; Jefferson Medical Hospital, Philadelphia, Pa.; Buffalo General, Buffalo, N.Y.; St. Francis Hospital, Pittsburg, Pa.; Walter Reed Hospital, Washington, D.C.; U. of Minn., Minneapolis, Minn.; Toledo Hospital, Toledo, Ohio; St. Peter's Hospital, St. Peters, Minn.; Hackley Hospital, Muskegon, Michigan; Practical Nurses Cap.

St. Lukes Nursing School, Marquette, Michigan; St. Alexis Hospital, Bismark. North Dakota; St. Mary's Hospital, Detroit, Michigan; Long Island College, Brooklyn, New York; E. W. Sparrow Hospital, Michigan State College, Lansing, Michigan; Wabash Valley Sanitarium and Hospital, Lafayette, Indiana; Saginaw General Hospital, Saginaw, Mich. St. Joseph's Hospital, St. Paul, Minn.; Broadlawn Polk County Hospital, Des Moins, Iowa; Natches Charity Hospital, Natches, Miss.

Mercy College, School of Nursing, Detroit, Michigan; (divisions also in Ann Arbor and Jackson); Michael Reese Hospital, Chicago, Illinois; Grace Hospital, Windsor Ontario, Canada; St. Joseph's Hospital, Mt. Clemons, Michigan; Madison Hospital, Madison, Tenn.; California Hospital, Los Angeles, Calif.; Memorial Hospital, St. Thomas, Ontario; Providence Hospital, Detroit, Michigan; Bryn Mawr Hospital, Bryn Mawr, Pa.

Nurses' caps once signified one's alma mater. *Courtesy of Ypsilanti Archives.*

departments. Doctor Russell Miller doubled as the paper's official photographer. The *Banner* contained monthly reports from all of the hospital departments, including X-ray, Dietary, Laundry, Maintenance, Public Health/Visiting Nurses, Lab, Housekeeping and Office. The paper also published editorials on medical topics, monthly features spotlighting one hospital department, political polls and medical humor.

Its editor, Joan Hooper, was serious about her job. In an article about a change in editorship, the *Banner* notes it "came out each month under Mrs. Hooper's guidance even in trying circumstances; for instance, on Aug. 30, 1952, she was married to Joseph Hooper, but the issue came out as usual. In the winter '53–'54 Joan became a patient of this Hospital and was ill for about two months, but the *Banner* came out on time. One issue was prepared, edited, and composed from her sick-bed."

3. The paper was democratic, and here is its charm. It did not offer puff pieces about doctors, at the expense of those with humbler jobs. Everyone received equal mention, from the student "tray ladies" in the cafeteria to launderers and lab technicians. One article notes that several employees received pins for faithful service, including Mrs. Minnie DeNike for ten years of work in the kitchen and Mrs. Judy Schrader for five years of work in the X-ray department. Another includes a photo of a bowling trophy won by cook Juanita Ver Vaueke and a track medal won by kitchen aide and college student John Oney. A third includes a photo of Tiny, a dog belonging to laundry worker Ruby Busha. The photo caption reads, "She's proud of the way he can beg for his supper by sitting up on his hind legs and prancing."

The paper even extended its coverage area outside the hospital walls to a bird's nest outside the delivery room. "We have been watching with interest for the return of our robins who have been with us for several years," says the article. "The nest is high in one of the trees on the east side of the hospital but to date the nest is still empty. Evidently a new family is with us, though as we have learned the employees of the delivery room have been enjoying the rearing of a robin family from their window."

4. The paper covered medical concerns of the time. The January 1954 issue examined the local incidence of polio. It included polio survivor and nurse Mary Ann Witwer's description of the disease:

> *In August I was one of 1952's 58,000 people stricken with polio. The symptoms—stiff neck, fever, nausea, and headache—were all undeniable and awesomely present...my throat became paralyzed and I was unable to swallow, but I was not afraid when the doctor told me he had decided to do a tracheotomy. The local anesthetic stopped any feeling of pain. But feel I did—the cutting of the trachea, the cold touch of the hemostats against my neck, the strange sensation of breathing from my neck instead of from my nose.*

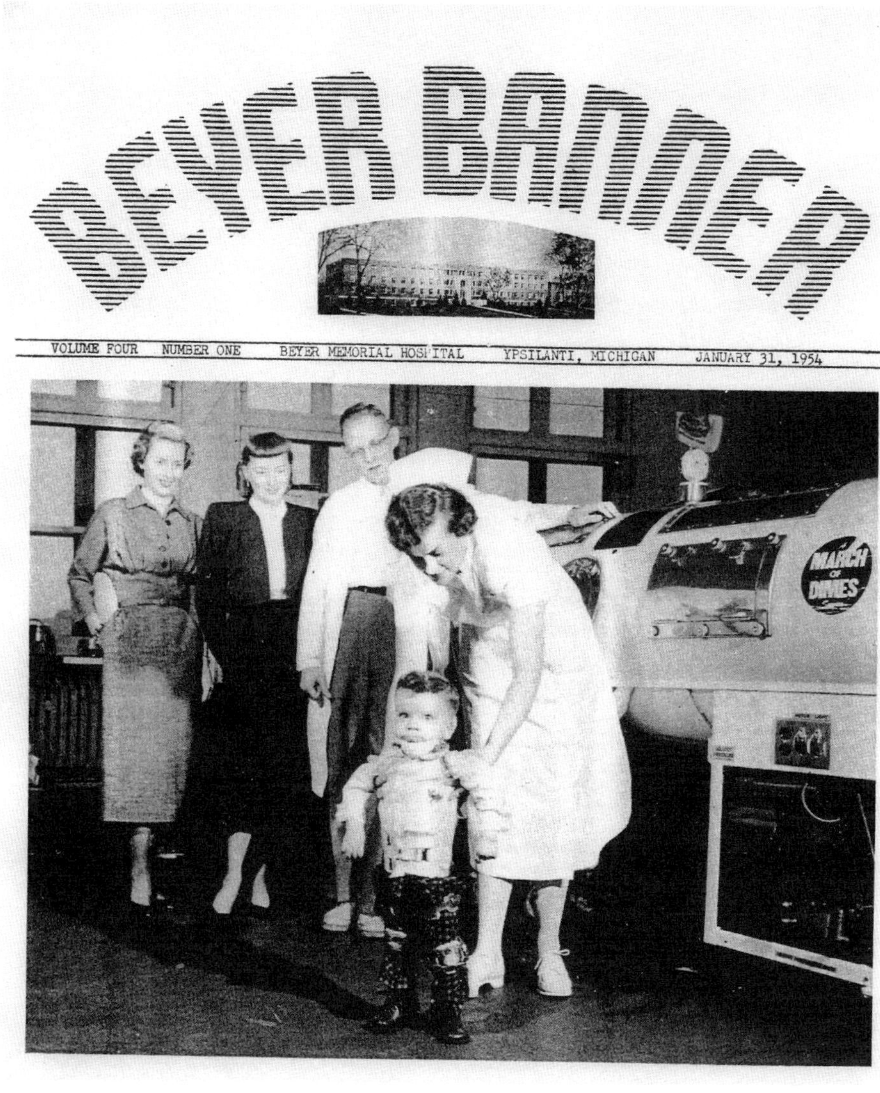

Some polio patients at the hospital were as young as five weeks old. *Courtesy of Ypsilanti Archives.*

The article also included three photos of children afflicted with the disease, one in a "pint-sized respirator," a miniature iron lung.

5. Last, the paper is peppered with medical jokes and humorous anecdotes. One story is titled "Happy Hospital Talk":

> *The conversational jargon of a big hospital is the strangest talk in the world. Listen to the X-ray technicians as they plan their day's work:*
>
> *"How many gall-bladders today?"*
>
> *"Four, and three stomachs; I can't help her even if she has seven chests and four hips. Let Mary do it; she has only three ankles."*
>
> *Wander up to surgery. An Attendant is preparing to bring a patient upstairs for an operation. He takes instructions. Then someone tells him, "Dr. Jones' appendix is in the lobby. And after that pick up Dr. Smith's finger from the emergency room, will you?"*
>
> *In the hall a group of interns are discussing an exploratory laparotomy.*
>
> *"Yes," one of them says, "Dr. Lawrence's lap is as good as new!"*
>
> *Down on the wards, the patients hear conversation about "Those cranks on the beds," and how they need oiling.*
>
> *While to patients, nurses may seem to be "angels of mercy," it's still surprising to pick up the phone on a hospital ward and have Dr. Whosit's voice from surgery say, "Hey, nurse, is my tonsil on your wing?"*
>
> *Yes, every profession has its own peculiar vocabulary, but the lingo of a hospital is just about the queerest conversation of all.*

Thanks to the *Banner*, those conversations—and a sense of the close-knit, affectionate hospital community that gave rise to them—are preserved in the half-century-old copies of this scrappy little home-made paper.

LIGHTS OUT AND STUD BUNNIES

As modern-day Washtenaw County residents cope with a recession, their thrift and sacrifices evoke the past.

This World War I–era flier details a conservation effort mandated by U.S. Fuel Administrator H.A. Garfield. If Ypsilantians ignored it, they risked losing the city's allotment of coal:

> *1. Light used for illuminating or displaying advertisements, announcements or signs, or for the external adornment of any building, or any unnecessary illumination of theatre entrances, shall be entirely discontinued on Monday and Tuesday of each week.*

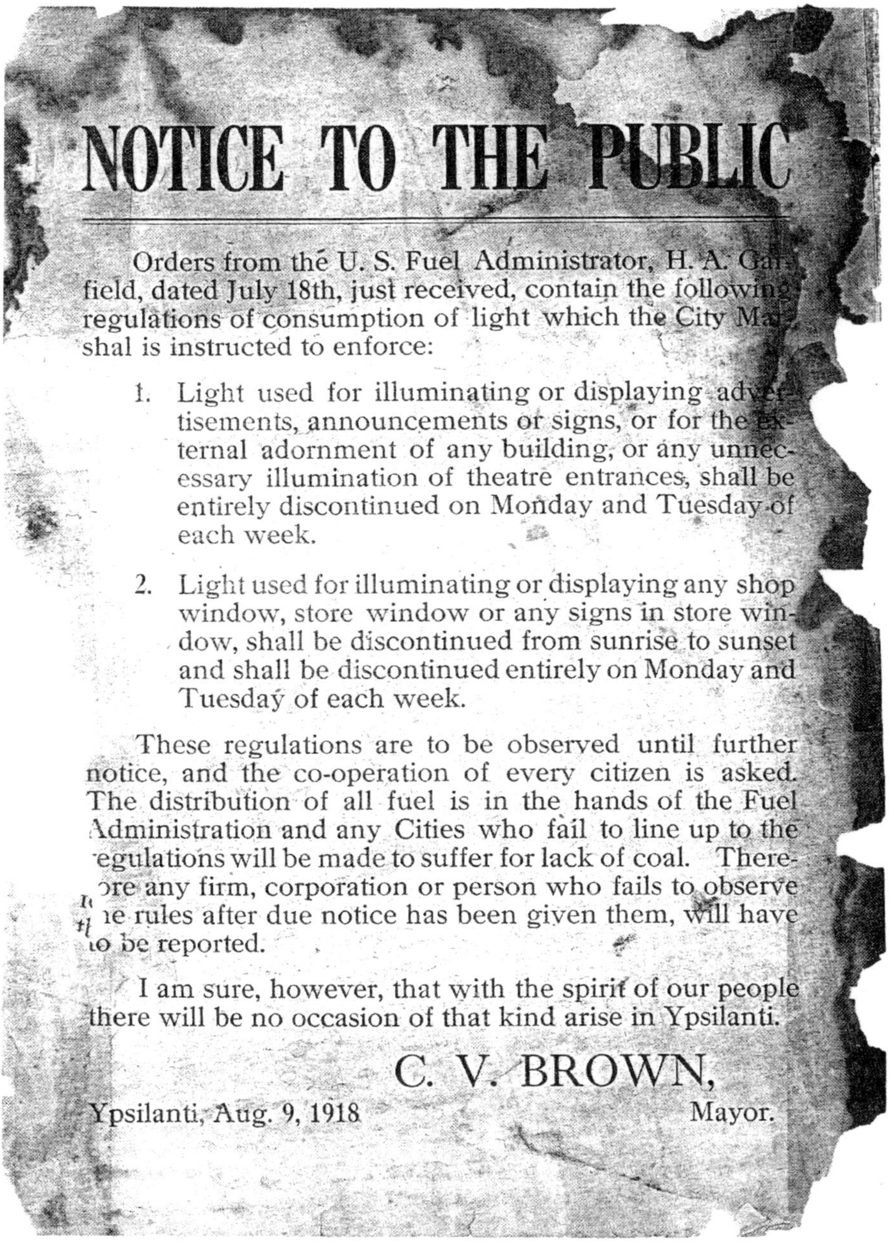

NOTICE TO THE PUBLIC

Orders from the U. S. Fuel Administrator, H. A. Garfield, dated July 18th, just received, contain the following regulations of consumption of light which the City Marshal is instructed to enforce:

1. Light used for illuminating or displaying advertisements, announcements or signs, or for the external adornment of any building, or any unnecessary illumination of theatre entrances, shall be entirely discontinued on Monday and Tuesday of each week.

2. Light used for illuminating or displaying any shop window, store window or any signs in store window, shall be discontinued from sunrise to sunset and shall be discontinued entirely on Monday and Tuesday of each week.

These regulations are to be observed until further notice, and the co-operation of every citizen is asked. The distribution of all fuel is in the hands of the Fuel Administration and any Cities who fail to line up to the regulations will be made to suffer for lack of coal. Therefore any firm, corporation or person who fails to observe the rules after due notice has been given them, will have to be reported.

I am sure, however, that with the spirit of our people there will be no occasion of that kind arise in Ypsilanti.

C. V. BROWN,

Ypsilanti, Aug. 9, 1918 Mayor.

In addition to light conservation, those violating emergency blackout provisions could be fined and jailed. *Courtesy of Ypsilanti Archives.*

> *2. Light used for illuminating or displaying any shop window, store window or any signs in store window, shall be discontinued from sunrise to sunset and shall be discontinued entirely on Monday and Tuesday of each week.*
>
> *...The distribution of all fuel is in the hands of the Fuel Administration and any Cities who fail to line up to the regulations will be made to suffer for lack of coal. Therefore any firm, corporation or person who fails to observe the rules after due notice has been given them, will have to be reported.*

In this spirit of wartime thrift, endorsed by no less an authority than President Wilson, one Ypsilantian asked city council if he could keep a pig in his backyard. His request "placed the city council somewhat in the position

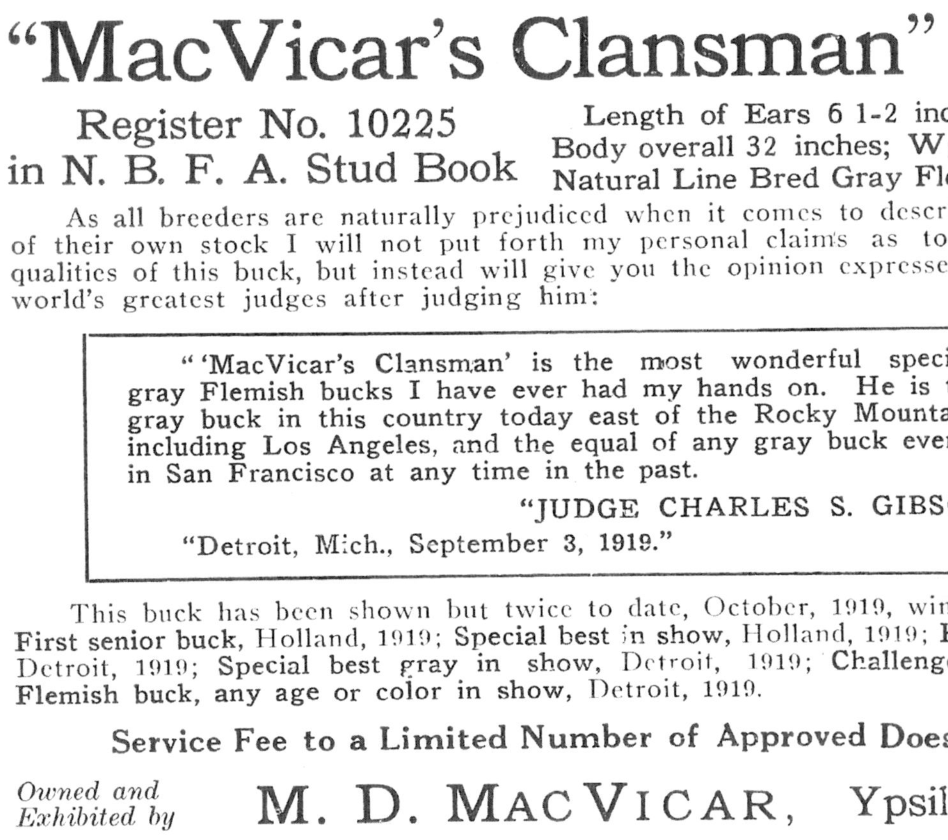

Does had to be approved. *Courtesy of Ypsilanti Archives.*

characterized as 'between the devil and the deep sea,'" noted the June 20, 1918 *Ypsilanti Record*, "since President Wilson has petitioned every citizen to do that which the City Ordinances expressly forbid." The council hemmed and hawed and shuffled the question off on the local health department.

On a less countrified note, a frontispiece from a 1913 Washtenaw County telephone directory shows an urbane young sales manager above several examples of the wonders of the then-novel Bell telephone system—and why its cost to the user was justified:

> *"A New Haven commission merchant recently telephoned the order for a carload of butter in Minneapolis, Minn, fifteen hundred miles. The message was received by the dealer in Minneapolis at one o'clock and by nine o'clock that evening the loaded car was on its way East."*

> *"A quick deal in real estate"; "A salesman for a Boston bond house"; "Immediately nineteen long distance Bell Telephone calls were filed in Pittsburgh to points in Ohio, and two to places in Pennsylvania. All the twenty-one calls were completed within one hour and ten minutes."*

The modern-day ease of calling someone, anywhere, was still a luxury in 1913.

Years later, during the Depression, some U-M students were doing without any luxuries at all. They toughed out privation without complaint, some enduring conditions, as noted by the December 8, 1932 *Ypsilanti Daily Press*, unimaginable to today's students. "Dozens of students…have only a bottle of milk and a loaf of bread for their entire daily diet. Many of them may be found rooming together in some attic at $1.50 a week, living on milk and bread or crackers and occasionally, a can of beans."

The *Press* continued, "Occasionally a member of the faculty turns in the name of a student who gives evidence in the classroom of malnutrition."

Three hunters in 1910 had the opposite problem—too much food. Ypsilantians Joseph Meyers, George Whitmeyer and Charles Rohn enjoyed their December deer hunt north of Iron Mountain. Their luck was so good that they decided, along with three other hunter friends in their party, to bend the law and exceed their hunting limit. But having come north on the train, how could they sneak the over-limit venison home, without detection by the game wardens prowling the train cars?

The men discussed the problem and hit on a solution. After shipping home their lawfully hunted deer, they'd take the best sections of the extra deer and pack the meat in a suitcase. The men soon boarded the sleeper car to return home with their baggage of illicit meat.

"The suit case was found by the wardens in the vestibule of the sleeper," says the December 19, 1910 *Ypsilanti Daily Press*. The warden asked the conductor to find the bag's owner. Detroiter J. Crossman, one of the hunting party members, claimed the bag but, upon arrest, denied ownership, "and a number of his friends butted into the game," says the *Press*. Crossman was taken from the train and straight to a judge, who fined him $20 (about $440 today). Warrants were later issued for the other five hunters. But how did the warden know that an innocent-looking suitcase was filled with a guilty cargo?

One hint may be found in the *Press*'s headline for the story: "Things Do Leak Out."

Eclipsing any shame the city felt to have its poachers singled out was the eminence of one tiny, long-eared Ypsilantian, the stud bunny

"MacVicar's Clansman." No less a personage than Detroit judge Charles S. Gibson offered a testimonial: "'MacVicar's Clansman' is the most wonderful specimen of gray Flemish bucks I have ever had my hands on" (which does make one wonder why a busy judge is running around handling rabbits). The sixteen-pound rabbit was noted for a long, sinuous body, which a photo caption takes care to point out is foreshortened in the picture. "Service Fee to a Limited Number of Approved Does, $12" (about $150 today).

THE UTTER CONFUSION OF CHOOSING A CALLING PLAN IN 1913 YPSILANTI

Like one of them new-fangled phones? OK, but you have to choose a calling plan. How about this one?

> *NON-GUARANTEE SERVICE. Calling party deposits nickel five-cent piece* [as opposed to the nickel ten-cent piece] *for each local call. Subscriber agrees to redeem slugs or other tokens deposited as nickels. Subscriber shall receive fifty per cent commission on receipts from local calls and ten per cent commission on receipts from long distance messages over the lines of the Michigan State Telephone Company, the commission not to exceed ten cents on any one message.*

Huh?

OK, well, that plan is out since it's gibberish. How about this one?

> *GUARANTEE SERVICE. Subscriber deposits five cents for each local call and guarantees amount inserted in contract for local calls. Also agrees to redeem slugs or other tokens. Excess local receipts to be equally divided, Subscriber and Company each receiving fifty per cent.*

Not much clearer. Note the stern warnings against slugs—clearly this was a big problem as people tried to cheat. One wonders how it worked. Was there a sort of pay phone right in your house? Or just a regular old cardboard box where you put a nickel in every time you called? Bewildering.

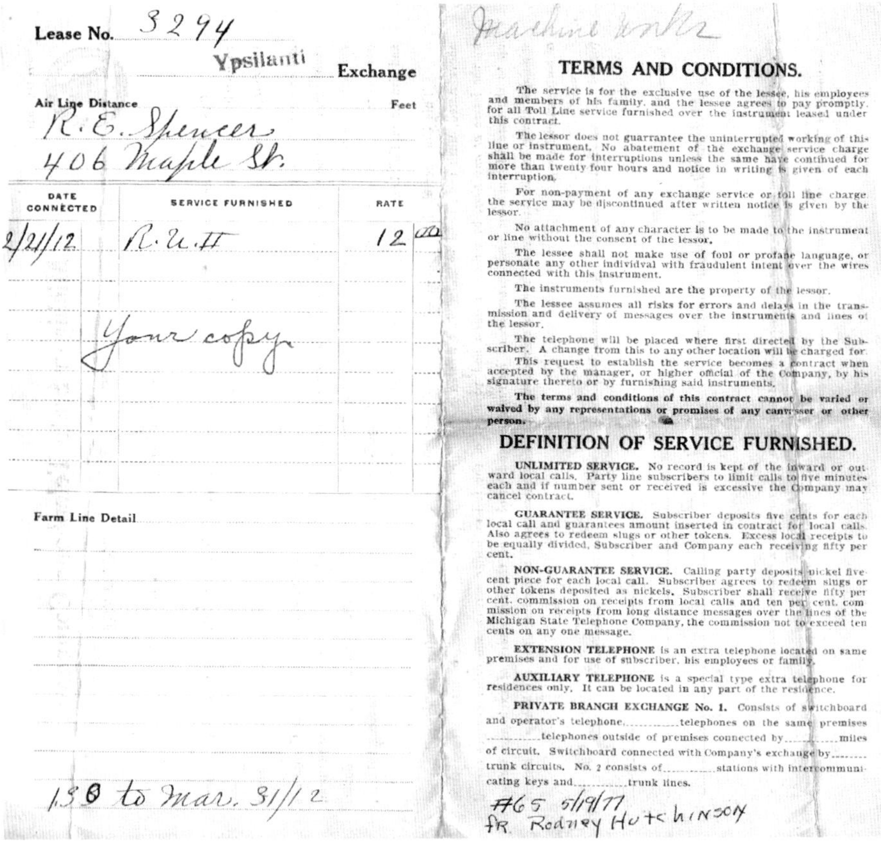

Lease No. 3294

Ypsilanti Exchange

Air Line Distance ... Feet

R. E. Spencer
406 Maple St.

DATE CONNECTED	SERVICE FURNISHED	RATE
2/21/12	R. U. II	12 00

Your copy

Farm Line Detail

1.30 to Mar. 31/12

Machine works

TERMS AND CONDITIONS.

The service is for the exclusive use of the lessee, his employees and members of his family, and the lessee agrees to pay promptly for all Toll Line service furnished over the instrument leased under this contract.

The lessor does not guarrantee the uninterrupted working of this line or instrument. No abatement of the exchange service charge shall be made for interruptions unless the same have continued for more than twenty four hours and notice in writing is given of each interruption.

For non-payment of any exchange service or toll line charge the service may be discontinued after written notice is given by the lessor.

No attachment of any character is to be made to the instrument or line without the consent of the lessor.

The lessee shall not make use of foul or profane language, or personate any other individval with fraudulent intent over the wires connected with this instrument.

The instruments furnished are the property of the lessor.

The lessee assumes all risks for errors and delays in the transmission and delivery of messages over the instruments and lines of the lessor.

The telephone will be placed where first directed by the Subscriber. A change from this to any other location will be charged for.

This request to establish the service becomes a contract when accepted by the manager, or higher official of the Company, by his signature thereto or by furnishing said instruments.

The terms and conditions of this contract cannot be varied or waived by any representations or promises of any canvasser or other person.

DEFINITION OF SERVICE FURNISHED.

UNLIMITED SERVICE. No record is kept of the inward or outward local calls. Party line subscribers to limit calls to five minutes each and if number sent or received is excessive the Company may cancel contract.

GUARANTEE SERVICE. Subscriber deposits five cents for each local call and guarantees amount inserted in contract for local calls. Also agrees to redeem slugs or other tokens. Excess local receipts to be equally divided, Subscriber and Company each receiving fifty per cent.

NON-GUARANTEE SERVICE. Calling party deposits nickel five-cent piece for each local call. Subscriber agrees to redeem slugs or other tokens deposited as nickels. Subscriber shall receive fifty per cent. commission on receipts from local calls and ten per cent. commission on receipts from long distance messages over the lines of the Michigan State Telephone Company, the commission not to exceed ten cents on any one message.

EXTENSION TELEPHONE is an extra telephone located on same premises and for use of subscriber, his employees or family.

AUXILIARY TELEPHONE is a special type extra telephone for residences only. It can be located in any part of the residence.

PRIVATE BRANCH EXCHANGE No. 1. Consists of switchboard and operator's telephone.............telephones on the same premises.............telephones outside of premises connected by.............miles of circuit. Switchboard connected with Company's exchange by.........trunk circuits. No. 2 consists of.............stations with intercommunicating keys and.............trunk lines.

#65 5/19/77
fr. Rodney Hutchinson

Subscribers were not allowed to use profane language. *Courtesy of Ypsilanti Archives.*

The Michigan State Telephone Company took a dim view of other hanky-panky, too, such as naughty language, the fifth item in the list of "Terms and Conditions": "The lessee shall not make use of foul or profane language, or personate any other individual with fraudulent intent over the wires connected with this instrument."

My favorite part of this contract? The awkward/charming way the MSTC tried to sell you an additional house phone: "AUXILIARY TELEPHONE is a special type extra telephone for residences only. It can be located in any part of the residence."

A special type extra telephone! Ooh.

But none of this fazed R.E. Spencer of 406 Maple Street in Ypsilanti in 1913. He signed the contract and was soon chatting away.

The "Naturo" Is the Newest Development in Constructing Closet Bowls

One evening, my husband tried in vain to do some work on his laptop at the dining room table but was inveigled into a conversation about turn-of-the-century toilet bowls.

Me: "Ooohhh...(demurely)...'Closet Bowls.'"

Him: "A bowl in a closet?"

Me: "Nooo, honey, this is a new innovation—it's a, y'know, *closet* bowl."

Him: "Oh, a water closet bowl."

Me: "Nooo!—even that is TMI, and this was a non-TMI age. This is a new technology. It has a slanted seat, for hygiene!"

Him: "Hm" (the sound of rapt fascination, so I press on).

Me: "Look—'The slanted Seat pleases Physicians.' See, even the logo is slanted—'NA-Tu-ro.' This is very High-Tech!"

Him: "Except it's lower tech on one side."

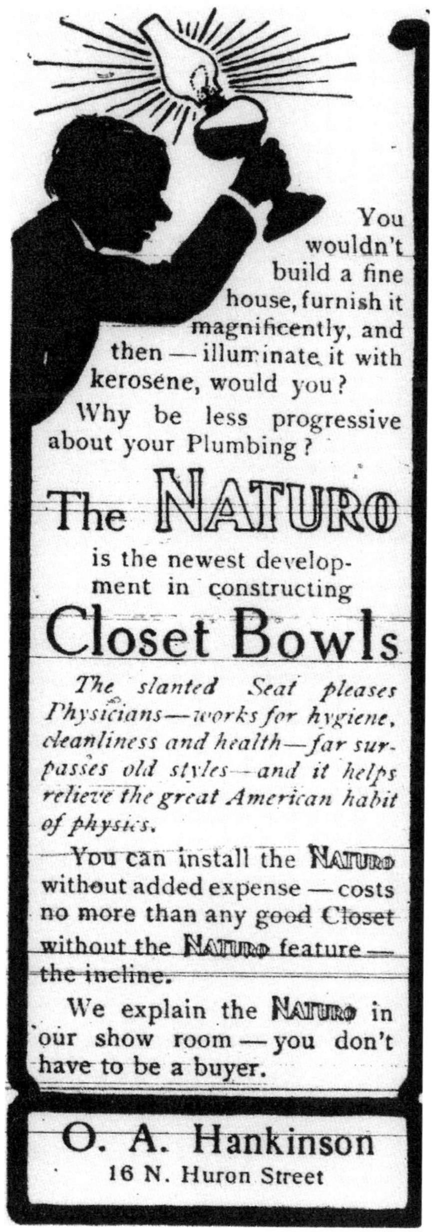

Feeling a little off-kilter in the bathroom.

TRIPE MONGERS MALIGN YPSILANTI-ESE

When in October of 1950 Ypsilantians were accused of "sloppy speech," the *Ypsilanti Daily Press* thundered forth with a series of four stories over six days that crushed, decimated and obliterated this ridiculous charge.

Under the headline "Jeepers, Wha'hoppin, Getta load of this! Precise Diction of City Unappreciated," the October 12 paper said, "Ypsilanti was today dubbed with the name of being one of the five cities in America with the 'sloppiest speech.' The charge was brought by the Linguaphone Institute of America which claims that it made a survey and found that the people in Ypsilanti 'just don't seem to care about their speech.'"

Ypsilanti was not alone. "Other cities named were Brooklyn, N.Y., with the most 'sloppy speech' patterns," noted the *Press*. "Atlanta, Georgia, was named because 'its speech patterns are typical of the lazy south'; Chicago, Illinois, because 'most people sound like they are either being chased by gangsters or are running for trains'; Hollywood, California, because 'they sound as if they are talking with hot potatoes in their mouths.'"

The paper took a flinty-eyed look at the accusers:

> *It was learned today that the Linguaphone Institute is primarily interested in selling the Linguaphone. This is a machine that attempts to teach people correct enunciation through the use of records. The company normally "plugs" the idea of learning foreign languages via this method, but now seems to be going into the business of teaching people to speak English.*
>
> *Evidently, they sent a team to Ypsilanti where some 100 speech records were made. About 75 percent of these were street interviews and the rest were made in private homes. The other 17,900 people residing in the city were therefore not contacted or recorded.*

The *Press* was only warming up. It now targeted the word in question. "'Wet, so as to spatter easily,' is the definition Webster's Dictionary gives the word 'sloppy.' The institute making the charge must think that everyone in these five cities, so branded, speaks with a mouth full of water."

"Like most other college towns a great deal of slang is originated in Ypsilanti," the paper said. "Some of it is good and humorous and easy to

A baseless charge throws the town into an uproar. *Courtesy of Ypsilanti Archives.*

use; some of it lasts while other sayings and quips have a very short life. It is like the fad of wearing certain colored hats and other gimmicks."

The *Press* continued:

> *According to the president of the Linguaphone Institute, Mat Sherover, "Sloppy speech is the continued increase of provincial and localized dialect." How this could be possible in Ypsilanti is a big question for it is readily admitted that the population of the city is now greatly made up of people from all parts of the country who perhaps never heard of the city 10 years ago. How then could they be "provincial and localized"?*

The paper contacted nine city officials and local educational leaders and sought their opinions on the charge of "sloppy speech."

Mayor Dan Quirk said, "We're too darn busy getting things done to worry about speech patterns." The *Press* added, "He said it didn't matter much whether we use Oxford or Cambridge English as long as we understand each other and fulfill our jobs in life."

Michigan State Normal College (EMU) president Eugene Elliott "pointed out that this area originally was noted for its fine speech," noted the paper, "but that a great influx of people such as Ypsilanti has had in the past decade [for bomber plant work] was certain to change the speech patterns. 'It is true,' he said, 'that the cultural pattern has changed and the language of the area has changed.' The noted educator, however, did not consider this as a criticism but as a statement of fact."

City Manager N.G. Damoose barked, "What hearing aid are they trying to sell?"

The following day, the paper featured a photo of Mayor Quirk. The caption read, "SCRATCHING HIS HEAD in bewilderment, Mayor Dan Quirk reads the charges that the city of Ypsilanti is one of the five worst in the country when it comes to speech. He is wondering just what the accusing company found facts on which to base their claim."

Also on the front page, two additional stories addressed the issue. One headlined "Other 'Sloppy' Cities Protest Too" offered an expert's opinion:

> *Professor Henry Owens of the language department of Michigan State Normal College merely stated, in typical Ypsilanti English, "The supererogative and gratuitous jeremiad resulting from a supposititious interrogation of the indigenous citizenry of Ypsilanti by cautelous*

artifices is ineffably nugatory. The prima facie evidence of slurring malapropisms and errata in diction thus adduced by the inquisitors is redolent of malevolence, of a furor scribendi inherent in such tripe-mongers, and may not be esteemed a veridical proces-verbal. Lese majeste toward the King's English is ubiquitous, not immured in a given locale. Nil desperandum."

The second story, "Ypsilanti Happy as Eve with Apple," said that Ypsilantians, whose pristine speech was naturally uncorrupted by slang, were now, just for novelty's sake, trying out the buzzwords of the day. The paper noted, "There seems to be a movement now to actually find out what [slang is] all about."

The *Press* helpfully spelled out the meanings of some of these unfamiliar expressions:

For instance, "getting a charge" is an expression which usually means that something makes you feel good and you laugh; a "big deal" means that something "great" has happened or will happen; "wha' hoppin?" is an expression originated by Great Godfrey which is simply slurring "what happened"; "hi, ya all" is used as a gleeful greeting which was brought from the South; "how ya doin'" means just that; "whaddya know" is just an exclamation used at a time of amazement or even as a greeting between friends; the other person usually says "nothin" and they go on from there; "on the ball" means that everything is all right or excellent in your estimation; "not so red hot" is the opposite of "really on the ball" and means the subject isn't doing so well; "cat's pajamas" did not die out 20 years ago, and it means wonderful or "swell"; "real sharp" is used mostly when a person expresses his ideas on an article of clothing that he likes very much.

The next Tuesday, October 17, the paper trumpeted one final blast on the subject, headlined "Note: City Does Care!"

Few groups have labored harder for precise selection of words than city council Monday night when it spent nearly three quarters of an hour determining proper language in the minutes of the former meeting. At issue was whether it had been "verbally agreed" to follow recommendations of the city manager with regard to use of voting machines in the

November election or whether it had been "resolved" to follow the recommendations.

Arguments were weighty on both sides.

And with that, the paper rested its case, having thoroughly vindicated its readers of the preposterous charge of "sloppy speech."

LITTLE OLD LADIES IN THE "UNDERWEAR CLUB," 1941

Every self-respecting Ypsilantian is familiar with the onetime Underwear Factory that used to stand at the southwest corner of Forest Avenue and the river. The site is now a parking lot. The building's giant painted mural of a curvaceous lady, clad only in a union suit, used to shock or delight passersby on the southbound train pulling into the depot.

But did you know that after the Ypsilanti underwear factory closed in the early 1900s, former workers met for reunions for at least ten years, from 1931 to 1941, in Prospect Park?

The workers formed a club and elected officers, and every August they went to the park for a big potluck picnic. Donations were requested each year to cover the cost of the reunions' modest yet special treat, ice cream.

At first, about one hundred people were showing up each year. But the reunions were dealt a blow when bad weather at the fifth reunion, in 1936, halved the number of attendees. For the following reunions, only about fifty people came. The newspaper clippings in the archives trail off around World War II, so it's possible that the reunions did, too.

At the tenth and possibly final reunion in 1941, a full generation after the factory closed, members arrived from Milan, River Rouge, Whitmore Lake, Illinois, Indiana and Los Angeles. A higher number of deaths than at previous meetings was reported. Members of the Underwear Club were passing out of this life but not out of history. Longtime club officer Sara Schaff hand-wrote an extensive, detailed history of the factory, including its multiple dam breaks and its destruction. Here is the (lightly edited) history that Ms. Schaff read to the club:

Train passengers made sure to look at the factory's racy union-suit mural, in order to be properly scandalized. *Courtesy of Ypsilanti Archives.*

The "club" gathers in Prospect Park in this undated photo, likely from the 1930s. *Courtesy of Ypsilanti Archives.*

Dear friends,

Thinking you would be interested in the history of the old mill I have prepared some items which I hope you will all appreciate and remember.

In the year 1827 a rude dam was built across the Huron River just south of what is now known as Forest Avenue Bridge. It was constructed of stumps, logs, stones, sod, and mud to hold back the water for power for the flour mill that was built on the site where the knitting mills and carding factory later stood.

This flour mill was called the Eagle Flour Mills and was sold to John Gilbert with the water power rights in 1839. Later in 1856 it was sold to Chauncey Joslin and the same year it burned and was rebuilt on the same spot.

Jacob Grobs Brewery nearby was established in 1861, and a few years ago burned down never to be rebuilt.

The first dam was swept away by floods and a larger and better one built in 1832. This was later swept away. The fine dam built some twenty five years ago was washed away during the great ice flood in 1917 and never was rebuilt. Electric power was being used during the later years of the mill's usefulness.

The pioneers Mr. Follett, Norris, Chauncey Joslyn, Murdow, Mr. Conklin, and Mr. Le Quirk were some of the early owners of the mill and factory.

A saw mill once stood near the spot where the Knitting Mills stood, also two flour mills, early records of the City state. The erection of the building that has just been torn down was completed in 1866.

Daniel Quirk and Asa Dow were the builders and later sold it to Isaac Conklin. It was then called the Ypsilanti Knitting Mills Co. Mr. Murby and Mr. Harely or Haryly were later associated with the building. Mr. Murby did not retain his ownership long after the tragic death of his daughter who was drowned with her sweetheart Mr. Fred Graves while boating near the Peninsular Paper Mills a few days before they were to be married.

It was during the ownership of Hay and Todd that the Mill attained its widest and best reputation when they made fine yarns and garments from them.

Later it was sold again to Mr. Kneip and J.B. Colvin. Mr. Colvin came here from Chicago with two girls and much machinery and equipment and started and maintained for years successfully the Ypsilanti Underwear Factory, [with] *which you are all so familiar. They continued the manufacture of underwear of different grades and qualities, much silk thread being used that was imported from abroad that was knit and fashioned by hand-powered machinery into garments, mostly underwear and some sweaters, of all colors and sizes.*

For two years or more garments were made that were later exhibited at the World's Fair in Chicago in the year of 1893.

The most expensive of these were union suits for a man who had them made to order (special) from pure [Japanese] *imported silk thread to take with him to Klondyke during the gold rush, and cost him $50 a suit.*

Much black wool yarns were knit into tights in those days. Many foremen have held positions during the years, also foreladies. In the 1890s about 250 employees were on the pay roll at one time. Many have come and gone, some never to return.

Mr. Pulver a night watchman met a tragic death while at his work there.

The Ypsilanti Underwear Factory failed in 1906 and '07 and later the Oak Knitting Co. moved here from Syracuse, New York and occupied

The factory was the city's biggest employer of women. *Courtesy of Ypsilanti Archives.*

One gold miner commissioned a special suit of pure silk underwear to take out west.

the buildings conducting a branch factory here for some years; later finding it unprofitable, they sold it to the Brotherhood Maintenance Corporation. The Ray Battery and the Jordan Battery leased and occupied it for some years then it was closed and empty with windows boarded up an indefinite time.

As it was an old building with some walls cracked and unsafe it was considered a fire trap and was condemned by the state fire marshal as a fire hazard; [he] *deemed it wise to have it torn down so it was finally sold to Mr. Julius Sarko owner of the Arrow Housewrecking Co. of Detroit. He and his employees wrecked the entire building in nine weeks by hand during*

The workers enjoyed camaraderie. *Courtesy Ypsilanti Archives.*

the months of May, June, and July this year. While doing so they came across some floors and walls of the old flour mills in the north east corner of the basement.

The tank and water tower were taken down by a Mr. Cody to be used at the Ypsilanti or Trojan laundry at the foot of Babbitt St.

The warehouse was taken down by a Mr. Alexander and the sheds and bicycle house were taken down by Mr. Oscar Ammerman who has looked after the property for some years.

Thus has passed into only a memory an old landmark which will long be remembered, especially by many gathered here today.

In the early 1900s, the underwear factory was by far the city's biggest employer of women. Without these hardworking ladies, the factory and its storied place in Ypsi history couldn't have existed. Here's a long-delayed salute to Sara Schaff and the lovely ladies in the Underwear Club.

"DEAR OLD YPSI: (MY HOME TOWN)"

In 1972, former Ypsilanti resident Lorretto Hughes Green revisited his onetime home. He wrote a memory piece that was published in a local paper and is here transcribed:

Aug 15 1972

Dear Old Ypsi: (my home town)

Sixty years ago when I left you, you were a nice quiet college town, population about 12,000. Today you are a wonderful city. Then it was the Normal now it is Eastern Michigan University. I was amazed at the beauty and size and number of those buildings.

How well I remember the town clock on old Central High. It faced all four directions. Many houses had summer kitchens and a wood shed in the back yard. There were hitching posts and horse blocks in front of them. Some things seem to be gone forever, as the blacksmith shops and livery stables.

There were a few cars there. If they wanted to take a ride on Sunday, they had to buy their gas on Saturday at a grocery store—no service stations then.

A young man courting his lady friend could walk to her house. They could go for another walk, stop in at the five cent show. The shows usually lasted about half an hour unless there was an illustrated song. That would be a phonograph record and slides. Down by the Old Mill Stream, Pony Boy and Smarty were very popular then. A five-cent dish of ice cream and home again…End of a perfect day.

A phone call—turn a crank. Central answered, "number please." "622J." "Line is busy." On a Sunday afternoon you could walk to Prospect Park. Most likely see a ball game. Joe Wilcox would be there with his popcorn stand, or walk up to Peninsular Grove, rent a rowboat, and ride on the Huron River.

Such words as disc jockey, baby sitter, panty hose, hitchhiker had not been invented yet.

Herb Shepherd cut ice west of the paper mill winter time and peddled it through Ypsi . We used to skate there too.

The Saturday night dances at the Armory with the Tony Whitmire Orchestra. The old D.J.&C. Does the famous paper train roar through Ypsi at 2:13 a.m. yet?

We would all be Senior Citizens now, but are there many there now who had Mrs. Yott and Miss Beardsley for teachers in 1907? And who worked at Peninsular Paper Company in 1911? I worked in the lower plaiter room there! A dollar a day for ten hours—very good pay in those days.

Oh the aroma of fresh baked bread around Gaudies Bakery. It always made me hungry.

Ladies wore rats in their hair. Their skirts five inches above the floor. Most men wore blue serge suits and stiff white collars.

Slang—"23 skidoo" and "Oh you kid." Stage jokes from 1911—An undertaker had a car. He converted it into a hearse. Now people are dying to ride in it. If the man in the moon had a baby, would the sky rocket?

We drove up to the end of St. John St. where I used to live and there I saw the object of my trip. That walnut tree my mother, Mrs. Thomas Hughes, helped plant many years ago. So dear old Ypsi as long as that water tower stands there and that tree grows you will always be my favorite city.

About the Author

Laura Bien is a graduate of the University of Michigan and Eastern Michigan University. She contributes local history articles to the *Ypsilanti Courier*, the *Ypsilanti Citizen*, www.ypsinews.com, the *Ann Arbor Observer* and the *Ann Arbor Chronicle*. She lives in Ypsilanti with her husband.